Alone in the Storm

Alone in the Storm
Leslie Vertes

THE AZRIELI FOUNDATION
www.azrielifoundation.org

Cover and book design by Mark Goldstein
Endpaper maps by Martin Gilbert
Map on page xxxi by François Blanc

LIBRARY AND ARCHIVES CANADA CATALOGUING IN PUBLICATION

Vertes, Leslie, author
    Alone in the storm / Leslie Vertes.

(Azrieli series of Holocaust survivor memoirs. Series 7)
Includes index.
ISBN 978-1-897470-88-6 (paperback)

1. Vertes, Leslie. 2. Holocaust, Jewish (1939–1945) – Hungary – Personal narratives. 3. World War, 1939–1945 – Hungary. 4. Holocaust survivors – Canada – Biography. I. Azrieli Foundation, issuing body II. Title. III. Series: Azrieli series of Holocaust survivor memoirs. Series 7

DS135.H93V469 2015   940.53'18092   C2015-906422-8

PRINTED IN CANADA

The Azrieli Series of Holocaust Survivor Memoirs

Naomi Azrieli, Publisher

Jody Spiegel, Program Director
Arielle Berger, Managing Editor
Elizabeth Lasserre, Senior Editor, French-Language Editions
Farla Klaiman, Editor
Elin Beaumont, Senior Educational Outreach and Events Coordinator
Catherine Person, Educational Outreach and Events Coordinator,
    Quebec and French Canada
Marc-Olivier Cloutier, Educational Outreach and Events Assistant,
    Quebec and French Canada
Tim MacKay, Digital Platform Manager
Elizabeth Banks, Digital Asset and Archive Curator
Susan Roitman, Office Manager (Toronto)
Mary Mellas, Executive Assistant and Human Resources (Montreal)

Mark Goldstein, Art Director
François Blanc, Cartographer
Bruno Paradis, Layout, French-language editions

Contents

Series Preface: In their own words. . .

In telling these stories, the writers have liberated themselves. For so many years we did not speak about it, even when we became free people living in a free society. Now, when at last we are writing about what happened to us in this dark period of history, knowing that our stories will be read and live on, it is possible for us to feel truly free. These unique historical documents put a face on what was lost, and allow readers to grasp the enormity of what happened to six million Jews – one story at a time.

David J. Azrieli, C.M., C.Q., M.Arch
Holocaust survivor and founder, The Azrieli Foundation

Since the end of World War II, over 30,000 Jewish Holocaust survivors have immigrated to Canada. Who they are, where they came from, what they experienced and how they built new lives for themselves and their families are important parts of our Canadian heritage. The Azrieli Foundation's Holocaust Survivor Memoirs Program was established to preserve and share the memoirs written by those who survived the twentieth-century Nazi genocide of the Jews of Europe and later made their way to Canada. The program is guided by the conviction that each survivor of the Holocaust has a remarkable story to tell, and that such stories play an important role in education about tolerance and diversity.

Millions of individual stories are lost to us forever. By preserving the stories written by survivors and making them widely available to a broad audience, the Azrieli Foundation's Holocaust Survivor Memoirs Program seeks to sustain the memory of all those who perished at the hands of hatred, abetted by indifference and apathy. The personal accounts of those who survived against all odds are as different as the people who wrote them, but all demonstrate the courage, strength, wit and luck that it took to prevail and survive in such terrible adversity. The memoirs are also moving tributes to people – strangers and friends – who risked their lives to help others, and who, through acts of kindness and decency in the darkest of moments, frequently helped the persecuted maintain faith in humanity and courage to endure. These accounts offer inspiration to all, as does the survivors' desire to share their experiences so that new generations can learn from them.

The Holocaust Survivor Memoirs Program collects, archives and publishes these distinctive records and the print editions are available free of charge to educational institutions and Holocaust-education programs across Canada. They are also available for sale to the general public at bookstores. All revenues to the Azrieli Foundation from the sales of the Azrieli Series of Holocaust Survivor Memoirs go toward the publishing and educational work of the memoirs program.

～

The Azrieli Foundation would like to express appreciation to the following people for their invaluable efforts in producing this book: Doris Bergen, Sherry Dodson (Maracle Press), Barbara Kamieński, Karen Kligman, Therese Parent, and Margie Wolfe and Emma Rodgers of Second Story Press.

About the Glossary

The following memoir contains a number of terms, concepts and historical references that may be unfamiliar to the reader. For information on major organizations; significant historical events and people; geographical locations; religious and cultural terms; and foreign-language words and expressions that will help give context and background to the events described in the text, please see the glossary beginning on page 119.

Introduction

In many ways, Leslie Vertes's story is not unlike those of other Hungarian Jewish survivors of the Holocaust. Although he was only fifteen years old when Nazi Germany invaded Poland in September 1939 and launched World War II, he felt the sting of increasingly intensifying antisemitism, the pain of a bevy of intrusive anti-Jewish decrees and policies that gradually segregated him from Hungarian non-Jewish society – including barring him from completing his education – and eventually, the separation, loss and destruction brought out by deportations and death faced by millions during this period. Yet in certain ways, his childhood experiences and biography reflected particular and relatively unique historical realities for Jews in this part of Europe. Leslie Vertes's life after the end of World War II might be characterized as anything but "liberation."

Born in the small village of Ajak in 1924, Leslie moved with his parents north to Kisvárda a short time later. Kisvárda was a larger town than Ajak and offered his father, a shoemaker, greater opportunity to ply his trade and support their growing family. Leslie's sister, Barbara, was born four years later. Kisvárda had a relatively large Jewish community; Jews made up about one-third of the population and were highly represented in commerce and business in the town. This reality reflected broader trends in the economic characteristics of Jewish communities across Hungary and elsewhere in the region, a result of the exclusion of Jews from owning land and farming prior to their emancipation in the 1860s.[1]

Jews who lived in the Austro-Hungarian Empire, which existed between 1867 and 1918, fared relatively well due to the multiethnic realities of the state. Jews contributed greatly to the economic, cultural and social fabric of the Empire. In the Hungarian part of the Empire, Jews were encouraged to adopt Hungarian language, culture and identity in an effort to increase the number of Magyars (Hungarians) living within the kingdom. In exchange, they earned increased chances for upward social mobility. By 1910, a majority of the Jewish population considered the Hungarian language to be their mother tongue.[2] In the early twentieth century, Jews were over-represented in higher education as well as within the officer rankings of the Austro-Hungarian army, and many reached high governmental positions, signifying their deep acculturation into and identification with Hungarian society. Many Hungarian Jews identified themselves as first Hungarian, then Jewish.

However, alongside their upward rise, Jews in the Austro-Hungarian Empire faced increasing hostility in the form of a new political antisemitism, which combined strains of anti-capitalism, xenophobia and more "traditional" religious (Christian) anti-Judaism.[3] This mindset, which in time combined with the increasingly popular racial nationalism prevalent at the turn of the twentieth century, served to set up Jews as the primary scapegoat for all of society's ills. Pseudoscientific theory sought to prove the superiority of a Hungarian "race," and the blame for economic and social problems lay with the "inferior Jewish race," according to this ideology.

---

1   Zoltán Vági, László Csősz and Gábor Kádár, *The Holocaust in Hungary: Evolution of a Genocide* (Lanham, MD: Altamira Press in association with the United States Holocaust Memorial Museum, 2013), xxxi.

2   Vági, Csősz, Kádár, xxxii.

3   For a broader study of the roots of religious anti-Judaism, see Robert Wistrich, *Antisemitism: The Longest Hatred* (New York: Pantheon Books, 1991).

After the defeat of the Austro-Hungarian Empire in World War I and the October 1918 revolution, Hungary was ruled briefly by a Communist dictatorship. Some 60 per cent of the Hungarian Soviet Republic's leaders were Jews, either by religion or through their ancestry. And although the foundations of leftist ideology led them to renounce their Jewish identity, a persistent view among non-Jews took hold – that the Jews had orchestrated the communist dictatorship as an uprising against non-Jews. The Communist dictatorship was short-lived and in the summer of 1919, Bolshevik rule collapsed. Admiral Miklós Horthy, the last commander of the Austro-Hungarian navy, marched anti-revolutionist troops into Budapest and in March 1920, was elected regent of a multiparty, autocratic parliamentary system.

Following Horthy's election, a new wave of violence broke out. Rooted in traditional anti-Jewish sentiments and fuelled by misinterpretation of the Communist dictatorship as "Jewish rule," pogroms broke out across the country. Following the signing of the Trianon Peace Treaty of June 1920, bitter social tensions remained, exacerbated by the dismemberment of Hungary's territory. The Treaty drastically changed the social, economic and physical makeup of the country: two-thirds of the country's territory was meted out to successor states, and more than three million Hungarians found themselves outside of Hungary's new borders, in Czechoslovakia, Romania and what would later become Yugoslavia. This greatly disrupted Hungarian economy and society, cutting the country off from its traditional markets and tearing apart its transportation infrastructure.[4] Moreover, the reversal or at least alteration of the terms of the Treaty of Trianon became the central focus of Hungarian political rhetoric and policy for the coming decades.

The political dismemberment of the country affected Hungarian

---

4 Vági, Csősz, Kádár, xxxviii.

Jews, including Leslie and his family, in different ways. After the borders changed, more than half of Hungary's Jews remained outside the country, but their proportion within the population increased. In keeping with the Horthy regime's reactionary, counterrevolutionary aims, its ideological framework for policy creation stemmed from "anti-liberalism, anti-bolshevism and antisemitism."[5] Antisemitism therefore became part and parcel of state politics and legislation, and discriminatory measures limiting Jews in various professions and education followed. For instance, in 1920 one of the first anti-Jewish laws in interwar Europe was passed: the so-called *numerus clausus* law, which restricted the number of Jews who were allowed to be admitted to higher education in Hungary.

One of the first direct experiences Leslie's family had with this new hostile reality was related to the legal foundation of their existence in Kisvárda: the citizenship of many members of the family. After the Trianon Treaty was signed, Leslie's mother, Ilona, Leslie and his sister, Barbara, lost their Hungarian citizenship. Ilona (née Weinberger) Winkler had been born in Nagykároly, which now became part of Romanian territory due to the border changes. Although Leslie's father retained his Hungarian citizenship, the family struggled for years to become Hungarian citizens once again and eventually had to bribe the authorities in order to wrestle their citizenship back. Their experience was a direct reflection of bureaucratic antisemitism that infused both policy and practice.

After Leslie's father lost his shoemaking company due to a fraudulent business deal, in 1938 the Winkler family moved from Kisvárda to the capital, Budapest, where Leslie and his sister continued their studies in high school. Although the family struggled to pay the school fees, and due to rampant antisemitism in the school Leslie was rather isolated from his classmates, he was a good student and was poised to finish his studies in good standing. But three weeks

---

5 Vági, Csősz, Kádár, xxxviii.

prior to his graduation, the principal informed his mother that Leslie would not be among the only six Jewish students who were allowed to complete their education. Thereafter, Leslie focused his attention on apprenticing in his father's shoe factory, despite their increasingly tense relationship. The complicated relationship Leslie had with his volatile father runs like a leitmotif throughout his memoir; however, the knowledge Leslie somewhat reluctantly gained from his father's trade helped sustain him in dire circumstances, both during and after the war.

Across Europe, Nazi Germany spread its influence and reign by occupying more and more territory. Although Hungary began as a reluctant ally of Nazi Germany, between 1938 and 1941, the country was able to return to its primary political objective and "regain" about 40 per cent of the territory it lost due to the Treaty of Trianon. Stemming from a desire to "solve" the "Jewish question" in Hungary, beginning in 1938 a number of anti-Jewish laws and decrees were passed, further excluding Jews from intellectual professions and many sectors of the economy. These were a domestic outgrowth of Hungarian antisemitic politics, rather than the result of direct pressure from Nazi Germany. For example, the so-called third anti-Jewish law (Act xv of 1941), reminiscent of the Nuremberg laws, prohibited marriage and sexual intercourse between Jews and non-Jews. The 1941 census accounted for 725,000 Israelites (people following Judaism), and there were approximately 100,000 Hungarian citizens of Christian religion who were classified as Jews according to the racial anti-Jewish-laws.[6]

The labour service, to which Leslie and his father were subjected, became yet another tool of discriminatory policy instituted by the Hungarian government. The institution was rather unique within the history of the Holocaust. While Nazi Germany and its allies gener-

---

6   Randolph L. Braham. *A népirtás politikája: a Holocaust Magyarországon* (The Politics of Genocide: The Holocaust in Hungary), vols. 1–2 (Budapest: Belvárosi Könyvkiadó, 1997), 74.

ally barred Jews from military service, Hungary conscripted every draft-age male Jew in order to ensure their contribution to the war effort. However, because Jews were considered an "unreliable" element, they were assigned to unarmed forced labour in military units, carrying out construction work and other types of hard physical labour. The particularities of forced military labour service in Hungary also meant that in many communities, the elderly, women and children were left behind to fend for themselves.[7] Leslie was first recruited into the Levente, a paramilitary youth organization that prepared young men for military service. Similar to Jewish men conscripted into labour service, Jewish youths like Leslie were not actually charged with any useful tasks due to their "untrustworthiness," and Leslie carried out unnecessary physical work under the verbal and sometimes physical abuse of the guards.[8]

During the war years, large numbers of Hungarian Jews (especially the more Hungarianized Neolog, or "Reform" communities) put their trust in the longstanding tradition of Jewish-gentile coexistence in Hungary and the allegedly "chivalrous" character of Regent Horthy. While throughout Europe Jews were being deported and murdered en masse, the Hungarian Jewish community remained largely intact until 1944. Although the anti-Jewish stance of the government was clear, and antisemitic atrocities by Hungarian military and law enforcement agencies claimed many Jewish lives,[9] Regent Horthy

---

7   Tim Cole, "A Gendered Holocaust? The Experiences of 'Jewish' Men and Women in Hungary, 1944," in R. Braham and B. Chamberlin, eds., *The Holocaust in Hungary: Sixty Years Later* (New York: Columbia University Press, 2006): 43-61.

8   Vági, Csősz, Kádár, 46-61.

9   The number of victims of the labour service up to the German occupation is estimated between 20,000 and 40,000. In July 1941, close to 20,000 Jews – mostly, but not exclusively, Jews holding Hungarian citizenship – were deported to Ukraine by the Hungarian authorities where they were massacred by the SS. The government halted the mass transports in mid-August, 1941, due to objections

and his government denied German demands to ghettoize and deport Hungary's Jewish population. The Hungarian leadership's reasons were manifold. In the wake of Germany's increasing military defeats, the Hungarian government began to explore the potential of a separate peace treaty with the Allies, and Horthy and his circle were well aware that handing over the Jews to Hitler would deteriorate the Hungarian negotiation position. They also maintained that removing the Jews from Hungary would jeopardize the economy and its military production. Therefore, while the conditions for Hungarian Jews rapidly deteriorated during the war years, prior to the German occupation of Hungary in March 1944 and in the context of the "Final Solution" being carried out elsewhere in Europe, most Hungarian Jews lived a relatively "normal" life.

Many Jews were thus quite astonished when, after the German occupation of Hungary on March 19, 1944, Horthy ordered the army not to resist and stayed in his position, remaining in place even after the so-called Final Solution was launched in Hungary. Instead, Horthy appointed a new, collaborating government. By doing so, he legitimized the occupation and approved the deportations of Jews. Even the Nazis were surprised at the enthusiasm of the Hungarian authorities in their efforts to deport as many Jews as possible. The speed and the efficiency were almost unprecedented: in a matter of only weeks, the majority of Hungarian Jews were forced into ghettos or – in Budapest – so-called yellow star houses. Between May 15 and July 9, close to 440,000 Jews were deported – 97 per cent to Auschwitz-Birkenau. The overwhelming "success" of the Nazis in Hungary was made possible by the smooth operations of the Hungarian authori-

---

by part of the Hungarian parliamentary opposition and pressure by the German authorities in Ukraine, who saw the uncontrolled influx of Jews from Hungary as a security threat. In January 1942, units of the Hungarian army and the Hungarian gendarmerie murdered about 3,000 Serbs and Jews in the recently re-annexed northern Serbia. See Vági, Csősz, Kádár, 23–69.

ties, especially the Ministry of the Interior, which directed the public administration and law enforcement agencies (such as the police and gendarmerie). The commander of the German unit in charge of the "de-Jewification" of Hungary, SS Lieutenant Colonel Adolf Eichmann, was accustomed to heavy negotiations with national authorities. He had rarely seen anything like what happened in Hungary: his partner on behalf of the Hungarian authorities, State Secretary of the Ministry of the Interior László Endre, was so determined to deport the largest possible number of Hungarian Jews that the commander of Auschwitz, Rudolf Höss, begged Eichmann to slow Endre down.[10]

The Hungarian authorities' efficiency was all the more surprising since, prior to the occupation of Hungary, the authorities had withstood German pressure to hand over any more Jews. After the occupation, one might have expected a reluctant collaboration, but instead a zealous campaign began. The sharp contrast might be explained by particular Hungarian political circumstances: the political, administrative and intellectual elite was, in general, more antisemitic than the actual leaders of the country, including Horthy himself (paradoxically, a proud and self-declared antisemite). After the German occupation, the small but influential circle of those who had previously prevented any such action was swept aside, Horthy was intimidated and pushed to the background, and the mainstream – represented by Prime Minister Döme Sztójay – came to power. There was no longer any obstacle in the way of ghettoization and deportation. The "conflict" that occurred in other countries (the Nazis pushing to deport more Jews and reluctant local governments wanting to give less) began in Hungary only in July 1944, when Horthy – influenced by several factors – was reinstated and halted the deportations temporarily. The stopping of the transports came just before the deportation of the Jews of Budapest, largely sparing the capital's Jewish community. The

---

10 Steven Paskuly, ed., *DeathDealer: The Memoirs of the SS-commandant at Auschwitz* (New York: Da Capo Press, 1996), 45–46 and 241–242.

anti-Jewish drive then recommenced after the extreme right putsch in October 1944, when Horthy was removed after his attempts to negotiate a ceasefire with the Soviets, and the Germans replaced him with the leader of the Arrow Cross Party, Ferenc Szálasi.

Having reached draft age, in May 1944 Leslie was conscripted into forced labour service. He earned some privileges by relying on his knowledge of shoe repair, which he performed for the commanders in charge of his unit. He survived several months of hard labour, after which he escaped back to his mother and sister in Budapest. Believing Leslie's father to be dead, they had prepared their own flight from the city, back to Kisvárda, with the help of false identification papers. After adopting a false identity himself, Leslie navigated life in Budapest with caution and trepidation, constantly in fear that the brutal Arrow Cross would discover that he was Jewish in their random identification checks. He barely missed the deportations and forced marches of labour servicemen and other Jews from Budapest that were organized in October 1944. The Arrow Cross handed over about 50,000 – 60,000 Jews to the Germans.[11] Between October 1944 and April 1945, Arrow Cross units murdered thousands of Jews in Budapest and the provinces.

As elsewhere across Europe, the end of World War II hostilities did not come easily to Budapest. The siege of Budapest lasted several weeks, and Soviet, German and Hungarian forces fought street by street for control of the city before the cessation of fighting. Nearly 40,000 civilians were killed during the siege, including targeted executions of Jews carried out by the Arrow Cross.[12] Out of the 760,000 – 780,000 Jews living in Hungary in 1944, only about 250,000 survived the Holocaust. The largest group of survivors was in Budapest, with the next largest group returning from the camps and labour service.

---

11 Vági, Csősz, Kádár, lxiii.

12 Krisztián Ungváry, *The Siege of Budapest: One Hundred Days in World War II* (New Haven: Yale University Press, 2006).

Like other survivors, Leslie viewed the Soviets as liberators, greeting the "first Red Army unit with happy tears in our eyes." But Leslie's "liberation" was extremely short-lived. Within a matter of days, he found himself under the brutal guard of Ukrainian troops and was marched east from Budapest along with thousands of prisoners-of-war, where he was then locked up in several makeshift and other more established POW camps in eastern Hungary and then Romania en route to Ukraine. This was the result of the Soviet occupation policies. Hungary was a conquered enemy state and was treated mercilessly by the Red Army. Looting and rape of civilians was an everyday practice. Men were deported to slave labour into the Soviet Union and the authorities did not distinguish between civilians, captured Hungarian troops or surviving labour servicemen. It is estimated that more than half a million Hungarian POWs and civilians, including Jewish labour servicemen like Leslie, ended up in Soviet camps, where tens of thousands of them died.[13] As the marches and deportation wore on, Leslie was taken to the Soviet Union, where he performed backbreaking physical labour for two years before he was able to return to Hungary.

Leslie Vertes's memoir provides unique insight into the varied experiences of Hungarian Holocaust victims and survivors. It points to the "last chapter" of the Holocaust: the circumstances in which Hungarian Jews found themselves in 1944, which for most was so drastically unlike those of Jews in Germany, Poland, or elsewhere. And while new studies have pointed to a lack of strict distinction between the emotional and physical reality of the end of war and of post-war periods for many survivors, for Leslie, the aftermath of the war was perhaps even more brutal than what he had seen in the labour service and siege of Budapest.[14] This was particularly true in Hungary

---

13 Vági, Csősz, Kádár, 334.

14 For instance, see Dan Stone, *The Liberation of the Camps: The End of the Holocaust and Its Aftermath* (New Haven: Yale University Press, 2015).

and other countries that came under Stalinist control, which then endured suffering under brutal dictatorships, a resurgence of anti-semitism and further destruction of Jewish communal life for many decades to come. On being deported by the Soviets, Leslie has noted wryly, "We were in the wrong place at the wrong time." His words characterize the post-war circumstances Jews faced in Hungary more generally. The Soviet victory meant the end of a genocidal campaign against the Jews by the Nazis and their allies, but it did not mean the cessation of suffering for Vertes and other survivors. Rather, a new chapter in persecution, as indicated by the significant portion of Leslie's memoir dedicated to the post-war period, began.

Rarely did whole immediate families survive the Holocaust, but Leslie's did. However, this too should not suggest that the Vertes/Winkler family experienced a "happy ending" and that their lives re-sumed as "normal" once they found each other again. His mother, Ilona, and sister, Barbara, survived while not knowing about his fa-ther or Leslie's fate. They therefore left Hungary, eventually settling in Israel, and it took more than ten years for Leslie to reunite with them after the war. The story of their search for each other and reunifica-tion is a painful reminder of the number of families torn apart by the Holocaust and of those who never found loved ones again; it is also a brief glimpse into the tremendous yet often woefully inadequate efforts by various agencies and organizations to try to deal with the crisis of "displaced people" and refugees in the aftermath of war.[15] In addition to recognizing the sheer losses Holocaust survivors expe-rienced – of livelihoods, property, lives, homelands – Leslie's mem-oir speaks of families ripped apart and never healed, of relationships

---

15 See Stone, *Liberation*, as well as Gerard Daniel Cohen, *In War's Wake: Europe's Displaced Persons in the Postwar Order* (Oxford: Oxford University Press, 2011), and Jessica Reinisch and Elizabeth White, eds., *The Disentanglement of Popula-tions: Migration, Expulsion and Displacement in Postwar Europe, 1944-49* (Palgrave Macmillan, 2011), among others.

broken beyond repair, and a persistent feeling of displacement. Leslie encapsulates this by titling one chapter, "Homecoming without a Home," and in the passage where he reflects on his solitude: "I sat on a bench in the nearby park and watched people. They came from somewhere and they went somewhere. They came from somebody and went to somebody. Perhaps they were rushing home to their family. And me? Nowhere to go, nothing to do and nobody waiting for me. I was free and I was home, but I felt so alone. I wasn't feeling hopeful about starting a new life. What had I survived for?"

After returning home from Soviet captivity, Leslie lived in a Hungary with less and less freedom. As of 1949, a Stalinist dictatorship closed in on the country, marking another low point of Hungarian history. Leslie was eventually able to leave during the anti-Soviet uprising that shook the country in 1956. The borders were open for a few weeks, launching a mass exodus: close to 200,000 Hungarians, among them many Jews, left the country.

Leslie's story of survival, and his perseverance in regaining a sense of normalcy after the war, is devastating and, at the same time, full of hope. It raises important issues related to the experiences of refugees as they flee war-torn and politically oppressive regimes to seek assistance beyond their borders. Leslie points frequently to shreds of humanity that helped him survive during and after the war years and allowed him to eventually prosper, carry on a new life, start a family and successfully work and retire in Canada, where he and his wife, also a Hungarian Holocaust survivor, settled. His experience and identity as a refugee and immigrant meant that he was constantly readjusting to life in new situations. He endured homelessness and poverty, which were underwritten by an enduring sense of loss. These experiences did not end when he moved to Canada, but he was fortunate to have contact with family that helped him get established and stabilized there. Far-flung ties from around the world – Israel, Hungary, Canada and the United States – linked him across space and time to his past, and helped him survive and thrive into the present. It is a testament to Leslie's resourcefulness and determination that he has prospered, but as he acknowledges, he could not have survived without the vital assistance from empathetic individuals willing to sacrifice and help him along the way.

Now, Mr. Vertes takes great pride in being a Canadian citizen, is fully embedded in Canadian society and gives back to the country through volunteerism. Notably, he has emphasized that, "If I had the chance to go back in time and pick any place to live, I would choose Canada all over again." This pride inspires his drive to speak to local audiences, including thousands and thousands of Canadian students, about his experiences during and after the war.

Alone in the Storm will serve to situate Leslie's experience as a Hungarian Jewish Holocaust survivor, refugee and Canadian immigrant within the framework of Holocaust history, commemoration and learning. What is more, it will reach audiences who have not had, or will not have, the opportunity and honour to meet Mr. Vertes in person. His testimony is an important contribution to the historical record, one that should never be forgotten.

Dr. Christine Schmidt
International Tracing Service Archive Researcher
The Wiener Library for the Study of the Holocaust & Genocide, London
2015

Map

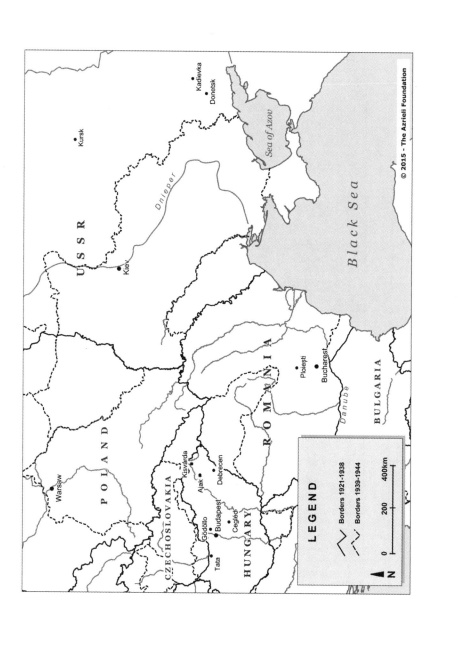

LEGEND

Borders 1921-1938
Borders 1939-1944

0   200   400km

N

Kursk

Kadievka
Donetsk

U S S R

Dnieper

Kiev

Sea of Azov

Black Sea

Warsaw

P O L A N D

CZECHOSLOVAKIA

Kisvárda
Ajak
Debrecen

Gödöllő
Budapest
Cegléd

Tata

H U N G A R Y

R O M A N I A

Ploiești
Bucharest

Danube

BULGARIA

© 2015 - The Azrieli Foundation

Leslie Vertes's Family Tree*

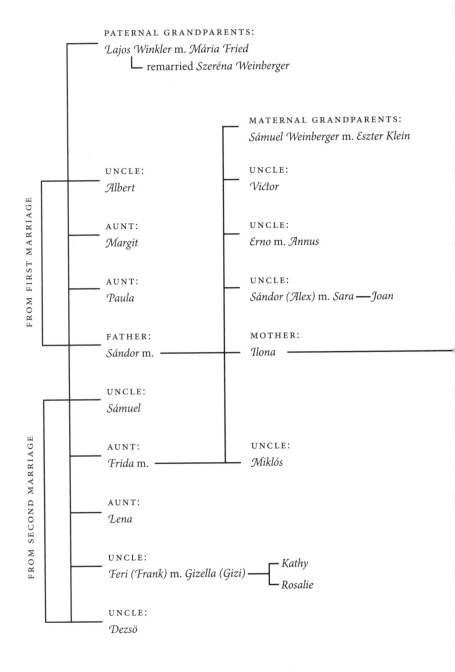

PATERNAL GRANDPARENTS:
Lajos Winkler m. *Mária Fried*
└ remarried *Szeréna Weinberger*

MATERNAL GRANDPARENTS:
Sámuel Weinberger m. *Eszter Klein*

FROM FIRST MARRIAGE

UNCLE:
Albert

UNCLE:
Victor

AUNT:
Margit

UNCLE:
Erno m. *Annus*

AUNT:
Paula

UNCLE:
Sándor (Alex) m. *Sara* ── *Joan*

FATHER:
Sándor m. ──

MOTHER:
Ilona ──

UNCLE:
Sámuel

FROM SECOND MARRIAGE

AUNT:
Frida m. ──

UNCLE:
Miklós

AUNT:
Lena

UNCLE:
Feri (Frank) m. *Gizella (Gizi)* ──
┌ *Kathy*
└ *Rosalie*

UNCLE:
Dezsö

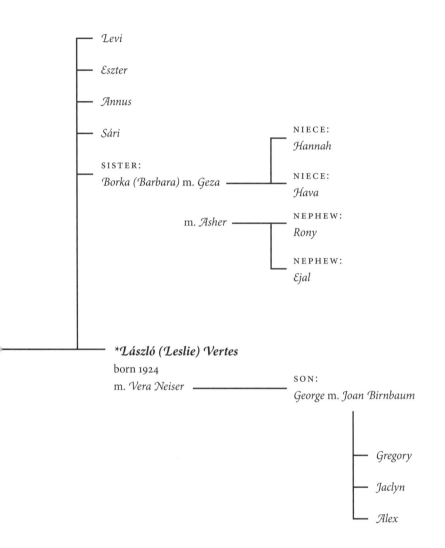

Levi

Eszter

Annus

Sári

SISTER:
Borka (Barbara) m. Geza

NIECE:
Hannah

NIECE:
Hava

m. Asher

NEPHEW:
Rony

NEPHEW:
Ejal

*László (Leslie) Vertes
born 1924
m. Vera Neiser

SON:
George m. Joan Birnbaum

Gregory

Jaclyn

Alex

I dedicate this book to the past, present and future:

To my mother, Ilona (Weinberger) Winkler, who brought me into this world and taught me right from wrong, instilled in me that, in life, not everything is black and white, and raised me to see the best in every person.

To my wife, Vera (Neiser) Vertes, who has been my partner in good and adverse times, created a family and a home, became my best friend and made me a better person. She helped me to recognize the real meaning of love, understanding, respect and appreciation. She also reminded me of small, but important, details, many of which I would rather forget.

To my only son, George, and my daughter-in-law, Joanie. They gave me three wonderful grandchildren, Gregory, Jaclyn and Alex, who are the tangible proofs of my destiny in this troubled world. They embody my hope that our family's history will continue, that our story will not end with the last page of this book and that my legacy will live on from generation to generation.

Acknowledgements

When one views a forest from the outside, both old trees and new ones are visible. When one enters, the individual trees stand out – the beauty of each one in its struggle to survive strong winds, insect infestations and heavy snowfalls. Just as every tree is different, so, too, is the story of every Holocaust survivor.

Thank you, Naomi Azrieli, for your leadership of the Azrieli Foundation's Holocaust Survivor Memoirs Program, which gives individual Holocaust survivors the opportunity to tell their unique stories. One of the best educational tools is a memoir – to help readers, young and old, Jewish and non-Jewish, see both the forest and the single trees within it.

Thank you to my friend Ervin Gross for his unlimited advice in bringing a semblance of order to my words; to my old friend George Glass for remembering the details of our time in the forced labour camp; to the members of the Montreal Holocaust Memorial Centre for their ongoing support; and to Arielle Berger, who read my original manuscript and chose to publish it. My biggest thanks go to my editor, Karen Kligman, who made a great effort to mould a good book from my messy pages.

Finally, I would like to thank you, the reader, for making the effort to see not only the whole forest, but also my tree with its growing branches. I hope that understanding the hatred and killing of the past will motivate you to fight for human rights in the present – to shape a better and peaceful future.

Prologue

I think of myself as having been born four times: the first time in February 1924 in Ajak, Hungary; the second and third times in November and December 1944 in Budapest, Hungary; and the fourth time in January 1946 in Kadievka, Ukraine.

Writing opened the lid of my box of buried memories. I had never wanted to open it before. Looking back at my long life's journey, I am dizzy contemplating the rough road and the distance I have travelled. Each page of this book carries the truth: nothing has been embellished.

Before I started to write, I did not envision much difficulty, but it turned out that the process was more than I had bargained for. In revisiting my past, I had to do a lot of thinking and research because I had forgotten some names, places, dates and events. While writing about some of these events I relived them, which was painful.

The Nazis and Hungarian collaborators robbed me of my youth. What they did to me, my family and millions of other Jews is etched in history with blood. Germany and Hungary, however, were not the only countries where antisemitism was rampant. There were others, including the Soviet Union and Poland, but the Nazis were the most organized, systematic killers of all. I still cannot forget what the Germans did, nor can I forgive the country of Germany, and I would never travel there.

The Nazis and their plan to wipe out the Jewish population swept across Europe like the wind, which picked up speed and force until it assumed hurricane-like properties. During my lifetime, I saw the wind blowing in different directions. I felt I was alone in the storm and powerless to stop it. I witnessed the immense prejudice and racism manifested by a growing number of individuals and entities worldwide. Unfortunately, no culture or civilization is immune to this sickness.

During the war, few countries and individuals opened their hearts and their doors to help the Jewish people. This fact shook my belief in human decency and still tinges my life with some bitterness. So many people died, including 1.5 million children and all they would have brought to the world. When we cried out for help, nobody listened – not friends, not neighbours, not even friendly nations. With their help, the direction of the killer wind might have changed. How many millions of people would still be alive today? They called their inaction "politics."

Can you stop the wind? While we cannot possibly stop the winds of hatred and intolerance, we can shield ourselves, at least to some extent, by taking certain actions. We can be vigilant and speak up against intolerance before it escalates. We can participate in organizations that safeguard human rights. Above all, we can stand up against prejudice, racism and bigotry in all its forms.

My memoir is part of my legacy to my family and a personal gift to my friends. I hope that my story also gives hope to others who are undergoing trials and tribulations. Without hope, life is not worth living. I fervently wish for my story, and the stories of other survivors, to provide a lesson that future generations heed: to listen, hear and help victims of persecution in order to prevent the repetition of our misfortune in the future, and to prevent others from experiencing what I went through. May their memoirs be happier ones.

A Shoemaker's Son

My father, Alexander (Sándor) Winkler, was born on March 15, 1902, into a large, poor family in Ajak, Hungary. He had an older brother, Albert, and two sisters, Margit and Paula. After their mother, Mária, died at a young age, their father, Lajos, married a woman named Szeréna Weinberger and had three more boys – Sámuel, Dezsö and Feri (Frank) – and two more girls – Lena and Frida. Lajos died before Frank was born. Szeréna raised the family on the small income she earned by doing housework for others and with help from Jewish charitable organizations. After his father, Lajos, died and his stepmother, Szeréna, fell ill, my father, still extremely young, learned the shoemaking trade out of necessity. Three of my father's siblings immigrated to the United States before the war – Lena and Paula in 1920, and Albert in 1937.

My mother, Ilona Weinberger, was born in 1903 in Nagykároly, Hungary. She had four brothers: Victor, Alex, Miklós and Erno. Victor, the oldest, became a decorated hero in World War 1. In 1919, he immigrated to the United States. Alex got married in Kisvárda and, in 1936, also immigrated to the States. In Hungary, Miklós married my father's sister Frida, and Erno, the youngest, learned shoemaking.

My parents married in March 1923. I was born on February 18, 1924, in the village of Ajak in the eastern part of Hungary. My mother told me that when I was only six months old, my parents' relationship became so strained that my mother ran back with me to her parents' home. Three days later, my father showed up at the front door, demanding his family. When he was refused, he threatened to burn the whole house down if my mother did not return with him. So we went back to Ajak. Six months later, our family moved to Kisvárda, a larger town with more opportunities for my father to make a better living. At that time, 25 to 30 per cent of the population of Kisvárda was Jewish.

My only sister, Borka (Barbara), was born in 1928. A baby had been born after me but died when he was only four months old. Then three more babies came, but they all died before they were six months old. My mother never wanted to talk about how they died, and my father said that it was none of my business.

When my father had to apply for Hungarian citizenship for our family, as did every Hungarian, he ran into difficulties. My mother had been born in Nagykároly, which was part of Hungary at the time of her birth, but it had become Romanian territory in 1920. Under the Treaty of Trianon, my mother was a Romanian citizen.[1] She had lost her Hungarian citizenship, and the Hungarian government, which I believe used every trick in the book not to grant citizenship to Jews, somehow used this fact to reject the applications of my mother, my sister and me, even though my father was a Hungarian citizen. It took some money from us, and three years of delays, before we became citizens of Hungary.

My mother loved to read, opening a book whenever she had a few free minutes. Even when we were short of money, we bought second-hand books. When my father turned off the lights around 9:00 p.m. to save money on electricity, my mother would light a candle, put it on the floor and lean over from her bed to read. I would sit on the

---

1 For information on the Treaty of Trianon, as well as on other significant historical events and people; religious, historical and cultural terms; geographical locations; major organizations; and foreign-language words and expressions contained in the text, please see the glossary.

floor near her bed and read as well. Thanks to my mother's influence, I have been reading all my life.

By the time I was ten years old, I had finished four grades of public school and was first in my class in mathematics, arts and literature, and last in gym and history. With my mother's encouragement, I continued my studies at the Bessenyei György Gimnázium, a high school in Kisvárda. I completed three years there. I became a diligent student and earned top marks in mathematics, science and arts. Since I did well in art class, my teacher asked me to join his after-school private course. I wanted to, but I did not have the money for extracurricular activities. The teacher offered me free art supplies and waived the fees for his courses. I really appreciated his generous gesture.

My father was a handsome, clean-cut man; in his work, personal grooming and attire, he was a perfectionist. He also had a good voice and danced well, especially after a few drinks. I learned a lot from my father. He was very organized and kept his work area spotless, and he insisted we all follow suit. He could also be rather cold, and he was a disciplinarian. I remember causing some trouble once by climbing over a fence and injuring myself, and the first thing my father did when he came home was slap my face, hard. The second was to take off his belt and administer one of his many punishments. My mother yelled at him, my sister peed in her dress and I begged for his pardon, all to no avail. When I was able to free myself, I ran outside to hide in the shed. During the next few hours, I heard arguments, my mother's crying and pleading, and the sound of slapping. These hours are still etched deeply in my memory.

Another incident I shall always remember came about through the kindness of a stranger so unlike my father. One hot summer day when I was about nine years old, I was on my way somewhere and paused to look into the window of a candy store, wishing I had a few pennies to buy an ice cream – a luxury we could seldom afford. A man stopped beside me, and as I started to walk away, he asked if I would like an ice cream. My face red from embarrassment, I said,

"Yes, but I do not have any money." He took my hand, walked into the store with me and bought me a chocolate ice cream. This warmhearted stranger inspired me to always help other people.

My father was an excellent shoemaker, and soon after we moved to Kisvárda, he started making ladies' shoes and boots for a large store. The owner of the store was a religious Jew by the name of Mr. Reisman. He paid for my father's first shipment immediately in cash, the next shipment in ten days' time, the next in thirty days' time and later on after sixty days. He then started to pay my father with IOU papers. My father had to sell those papers with a 20 to 30 per cent discount to pay his suppliers, to buy groceries and to pay overhead. All of these businesses accepted the papers as payment because Mr. Reisman was so well known and, apparently, trustworthy. One day, however, Mr. Reisman declared bankruptcy and did not pay my father what he owed him. My father had to scramble to get by, and the IOU papers became worthless.

One month later, the store reopened with a new owner, Mrs. Reisman, and the whole game started all over – the same system, the same method of nonpayment and shortly afterward another declared bankruptcy. Once again, my father was not paid for his work.

After my family lost everything in Kisvárda as a result of the Reismans' crooked dealings, we sold our belongings and, in the summer of 1938, we moved to Budapest. We rented a place on Szív utca (Heart Street) that had a large front room, behind which were a fair-sized kitchen and a bathroom. We divided the large room in half: the front part became the working and selling area, and the back part was our living quarters.

My father started to buy used shoes, which he skilfully repaired and then sold. In addition, he repaired shoes that customers brought in. It was a new beginning, though not very luxurious, and he earned little income in the first few months. But it was summer, so no heating was needed, expenses were low and we were able to survive. Our whole family helped my father as much as possible, and the business started to grow.

In September, my sister started school and I enrolled in the fourth year of a nearby *gimnázium*. Even though I was categorized as being in the lowest income bracket, we had to pay some school fees, which was very difficult for my family. The school supplies, mostly books, also cost a lot of money. I was always behind in the payment of tuition and other fees, but if I didn't complete the fourth year and graduate, it would be impossible for me to secure a well-paying job.

That year in Budapest was heartbreaking. The teachers, my classmates and the teaching system felt foreign to me, and when classmates found out I was Jewish, they distanced themselves from me. Although I had no friends and nobody to help me, I worked hard and, against all odds, got good grades. Besides studying, I had to help my father with his work in the evenings and on weekends.

In the spring of 1939, the principal called my mother into his office and told her straight out, "Your son is a good student, but he cannot finish the grade. One of the reasons is the unpaid dues." More importantly, he said, only six Jewish students were allowed to graduate and, as I had not started my studies in this school, I would not be one of them. The next day, just three weeks before the end of the school year, I stopped going to school. This was my first taste of systemic antisemitism.

Antisemitism had deep, historical roots in Hungary. Until 1867, when Jews became equal citizens, Jews living in Hungary were not allowed to own land or work as doctors, lawyers, engineers or government employees. Official and unofficial discrimination was visible in every field. The irony was that many Hungarian Jews thought of themselves as Hungarian rather than Jewish. In fact, the majority made a great effort to become "true Hungarians" and felt that they were Hungarians first, Jews second. In Budapest and other large cities, Jews assimilated through mixed marriages and by conversion to the Christian faith.

I began to spend my time at the shoe factory. One day, a well-dressed Catholic man came into my father's store to have some shoes repaired. He started talking to my father about going into partnership with him to produce new footwear for women. He would be a silent partner, financing the set-up, and my father would do the work, organizing production and supervising sales. This man, Mr. Trattner, owned an export company that bought, packaged and shipped goose livers to England. The less expensive parts of the goose were sold at the local market.

It was a good opportunity, and the Tatra Shoe Factory was born. Mr. Trattner rented a large main-floor apartment in Klauzál Square, and within one month we moved there. Inside, construction had begun, and machinery and materials started to roll in. In the front part of the apartment was a double-sized kitchen with a window. This became the finishing department, which my mother took care of, sometimes with a helper. The hall became the packing and shipping room. The largest room, with six windows, served as the main manufacturing section. Since the ceiling was quite high, a mezzanine was built, and this was where the shoe uppers were made. On the main floor, the sole-cutting machines and working tables were located.

Adjacent to the work area was our living area, a long room with windows looking out to the street. The front part became the bedroom for my sister and me; it had a bookcase, a writing table and eventually a small radio. The alcove, which had a full bathroom with a boiler to make hot water, was turned into my parents' room – without a door or dividing wall. Our living conditions were cramped, without much privacy, which meant I heard lots of arguments.

The business took off rapidly, with numerous orders. At one point, twenty-five people were employed. The business showed a profit even after the partner, the employees and all the expenses had been paid, and our income improved. My mother's brother Miklós and my father's brother Frank both worked at my father's shoe factory. It was there that Frank met and fell in love with Gizella (Gizi), a co-worker. Their wedding took place in our apartment.

One worker, a devout Baptist named Paul, played the violin whenever he had a few minutes of free time, during lunch or a coffee break.

I liked the instrument and enjoyed listening to the music, not knowing Paul was playing Christian songs. When Paul asked me if I would like to learn to play the violin, I was eager to. After a few sessions in which we used his violin, Paul gave me another smaller one, and I started learning to play by ear by echoing the notes Paul played. A few months later, Paul asked my father's permission to take me on Sunday morning to his church to join the small orchestra. My father laughed, not believing that I would be able to play in front of so many people. However, I did, and I was the only Jewish person in the congregation. Paul taught me some secular music, too, by Schubert, Liszt and Strauss. When Paul suggested to my father that he buy a violin for me, my father not only refused but also forbade me to ever play a violin again. He then fired Paul from the factory.

My father had asked me to work in his shop, but I refused to be under his dictatorship twenty-four hours a day. I had applied to other shoe factories, but nobody wanted to hire a competitor's son. I realized that it was time for me to learn a different trade. Because I was artistically inclined and could draw well, somebody suggested I become a printer and arranged for me to see the owner of a small printing shop outside Budapest, in Pest County.

The owner, a middle-aged Jewish man, hired me and started to teach me everything. Within a few days, I was able to pick and set the letters by hand, place them in the frame and use the leg-operated machine to print them. After a few weeks, the owner left me alone most of the time to take orders from customers and print small jobs like flyers or cards. Later, he started teaching me how to use the lithograph to print posters and business forms. My weekly pay was five dollars plus streetcar tickets and milk.

While I was working one day, one of the customers, Leslie Toth, came to pick up an order. We had a long, friendly discussion and after that, we often ate lunch together. He was two years older than me. His mother, who had died a year earlier, was named Ilona, the same as mine.

Three months later, my boss and I signed a three-year apprenticeship contract that included annual pay increases. All the papers were sent to the Association and Trade Union of Hungarian Printing Office Workers. However, shortly after sending off my apprenticeship contract, I was out of a job. No Jews were to be admitted to the so-called status trades, such as printing. In Pest County, the deputy prefect was László Endre, who would soon become one of the most notorious antisemites in all of Hungary. He supported laws against Jews buying land, opening new stores or factories or becoming teachers or government employees.

Having no other choice, I signed a contract with Mr. Trattner, my father's partner. My pay would start at five dollars a week, double the following year and be allotted per piece the last half year. Mr. Trattner was kind when he paid my salary, sometimes giving me a few cents more. Every other day, I went to a trade school before noon, and the rest of the time I worked in the uppers department, where the upper part of the shoes were made. I also joined a group called Self-Education, sponsored by the City of Budapest, which organized tours of factories, museums and palaces, and held interesting seminars. I learned a lot about art, history, architecture, geography and the universe. I remember my mother telling me, "If you do not know something, always ask! Only stupid people don't want to know; the smart ones are looking for answers."

Having been in the footwear business all my life, I progressed rapidly. I studied every single material: leather, synthetics, metals, textiles and glue. I also learned about the components' chemistry and about cost calculation. My main interest was the anatomy of the foot, and I visited footwear factories and hospitals to learn about foot injuries. My father was pleased with my progress, so much so that he deducted two dollars from my salary every week for room and board.

In 1940, my father was taken to a forced labour camp; the Hungarian government was drafting Jewish men into a segregated section of the army, where they were treated differently from gentiles. My mother and I ran the factory well; meanwhile, in his free time at the labour camp, my father spent money betting on card games, and on extra food and a lot of alcohol. He paid for these pursuits with IOU notes to camp guards, who came to us to collect the amount owed, plus a little more for their trouble. Paying off my father's debts, in addition to the cost of overhead and the partner's share, put us in a tight squeeze. When my father came back from the labour camp after about three months, he was dissatisfied with our financial situation, laying the blame on my mother and me.

Flowers and Forced Labour

Leslie Toth, whom I had met in the printing shop, was a regular customer at Mrs. Adorjan's dance studio on the corner of Károly körút and Dohány utca (Charles Boulevard and Tobacco Street). The dance studio was within walking distance of my home. Leslie took me there, introduced me to both the owner and head instructor, and paid for my first dance lesson.

I excelled at dance, and at the end of the first course I took, the studio offered me a position with a modest salary. It involved teaching in the studio three times a week and dancing with the paying students on Saturday mornings. On Sundays at 5:00 p.m., there was an entrance fee for ballroom dancing, but for me it was free.

During the day, I taught young girls a few basic ballet steps, as well as how to walk properly, for better posture. Evenings, I taught ballroom dancing to young adults between the ages of sixteen and twenty. One Saturday morning, a girl with a round face and nice figure came for the all-students' dancing, accompanied by her younger brother and a cousin. I found out her name was Ibolya Rosner. When my turn came to dance with Ibolya, she was shy in the beginning and a slow dancer, but we moved around and chatted away. This continued for several sessions until one day she introduced me to her brother, Andrew, and her cousin Tibor Weiner. They were polite, but had reservations about my fast-moving relationship with Ibolya.

I asked Ibolya to the Sunday dance, but she declined. On the following Saturday, the three of them came again, and I danced with Ibolya many times. She then agreed to come on a Sunday but only if the boys came too, which was fine with me. I lined up young ladies for them, which gave me the chance to dance with Ibolya most of the time.

While I walked them home, Ibolya told me about her family. Her father, János (John) Rosner, was a shoe repair supplier (it seems as if I moved around only within the footwear trade); he had a store on Baross Street, in the same building where they had a three-bedroom apartment. Tibor and his parents lived with them. Ibolya's mother, Kati (Kate), and Tibor's mother, Klara, were sisters.

John Rosner had a brother in Vienna who converted to Catholicism and cut any connections with his Jewish relatives. Kate Rosner's older brother, Ernő Neuman, lived with his wife, Anna, near Budapest in the township of Mátyásföld, where Ernő worked for a branch of Ikarus, a bus manufacturer. In order for Ernő to be eligible for promotion, the directors of Ikarus advised him to change his surname to a "real Hungarian" one and to convert to the Catholic faith.

In 1934, before their twin daughters were born, Ernő and Anna Neuman had become Mr. and Mrs. Nemes. They practised as devout Christians, and a large cross was displayed in every room. On Sundays, they attended church, and they celebrated Easter and Christmas in grand style. When their girls were school age, they enrolled them in the best parochial school, run by nuns. Later, when Ibolya's family and I visited the Nemes family, we avoided talking about religion.

Ibolya worked in an art studio, drawing faceplates for water and oil pressure gauges. We had a few dates, without escorts, and danced as much as possible. One day, after work, I had a free evening and decided to show up unexpectedly at Ibolya's door. Flowers in hand, as was my custom, I rang the bell. Ibolya was surprised, not because I had arrived so unexpectedly but because I had failed to shave before coming to see her. Although I usually shaved in the morning or before going to the studio, unfortunately I had not done so this time. Ibolya kindly asked me if I would like to return after shaving. I ran to the nearest barbershop, had a shave and headed back to her home, where I was welcomed most warmly. I learned my lesson: since then, I shave every day.

Ibolya, Andrew and Tibor were constant guests in our home, as we were in theirs. My sister, Barbara, and Tibor grew to love each other. Sometimes the four of us visited museums, but mostly it was just Ibolya and me. Concerts and operettas were our favourite forms of entertainment, and since we both loved nature, we hiked often that summer.

~

In 1940, the Hungarian government issued an order stating that until the armed forces drafted all men into the army, every male who was fourteen years or older had to report once a week to a paramilitary youth unit, called Levente. We were drilled as if we were in the army: we ran, hiked, fought and used old single-barrel rifles, and sometimes, in the advanced group, live ammunition.

In the spring of 1941, Jewish youth were restricted to serving only in certain auxiliary units, since they were not considered trustworthy enough for the country's armed forces. The government had created a specific supplementary labour service. Once a week, I had to assemble, along with other Jews, at a school, from where, after putting on the required yellow armbands and picking up some shovels and pickaxes, we went with armed escorts to a field outside the city. Along the way, people made nasty remarks about Jews, calling us enemies of the true Hungarian people. Some even spat on us.

We did unnecessary, dirty jobs – digging holes one day and covering them up the next time around. The four hours we had to spend there passed slowly, not because of the physical work but because of the verbal abuse from the armed escorts. They took every opportunity to humiliate us and play tricks on us, calling us "filthy, dirty Jews."

Among the young Hungarian soldiers was István, whom I called by his less formal name, Pista, as he had worked in my father's shoe factory for a short time. One day I was close by him and quietly asked, "Pista, can you give me a few minutes' extra break? I am not feeling well." His face reddened, and he slapped my face, kicked my leg and hit me with the shovel, yelling, "You dirty, good-for-nothing Jew! I am not Pista to you anymore!" Another older soldier, who had seen the situation, asked what it was all about. When Pista told him, he sent him to another post and gave me a short break.

I continued working while my father was called up again to report to a labour camp in the spring of 1942. German, Hungarian and Italian armed forces were fighting the advancing Red Army, and Hungarian army units were being sent to the Eastern front to serve. The Jewish units, however, were called to serve in the *Munkaszolgálat*, the forced labour service. Jews had to dig trenches and do all the dirty work. Sometimes they had to crawl forward to check whether a place was mined. Many died from exploding landmines.

When my father was away, it was at least a great relief for our family; there was less tension and we had fewer arguments. In the spring of 1943, I saw a poster calling for volunteer firefighters. I reported to the City Fire Department and was accepted for training a week later. From then on, I didn't have to go to the supplementary labour unit for Jews. The firefighter training was efficient; we learned how to recognize different causes of fire and when to use water, foam or another fire retardant. After one week of full-time training, about half of the students, including me, graduated and received official documents with our photos on them. I was assigned to a unit at the veterinary hospital. The rotating schedule consisted of twelve hours of duty – one daytime shift, followed by one nighttime shift – and twenty-four hours off. When my off-duty time fell during the day, I worked in our family's factory. The work schedule wasn't easy, but it was better than digging holes.

The City Fire Department had a portable, self-standing pump machine and a truck, and it supplied our work clothes and anything we needed to fight a fire. We practised all the time in order to be ready. The only time we faced a problem was during air raids, when we had to run several kilometres to the fire station in the pitch dark to serve as a backup team. We considered the possibility of falling bombs to be a small inconvenience. I was involved in fighting a few small fires and one huge one, when a fuel depot caught fire.

In 1943, the Red Army broke through the German lines and pushed the Nazis back from Stalingrad. There were numerous casualties. Some forced labour units were lucky to be captured by the Soviets instead of the Germans; others, like the one my father was in, broke away from the Germans and were able to find the partisans. Then they worked for the Red Army, doing similar tasks to ones they had done before, but their lives were not in immediate danger.

The Red Army advanced quickly, suffering heavy losses. They did not trust the Jewish refugees they came across and shipped them eastward, often to Siberia. The cold and insufficient food did not sustain them for long. Medical facilities were limited, for not only Jews but also the local people. In mid-summer 1943, the Hungarian government, unaware that my father had escaped, sent a letter of regret to my mother, informing her that her husband had died on the Ukrainian front.

During this time, my father's business partner was able to buy materials so that our small factory could produce men's boots for the city workers. My mother and I organized the production. I did the cutting and was able to save some material to produce a few pairs of boots for Jewish men who were called to serve in the labour service. Although our factory was busy, there was a shortage of all materials, especially of the leathers used in uppers and soles. For the uppers, we started to use pig, rabbit and dog skin instead, and for the soles, we came up with an innovation: We bought canvas and old movie reels made of celluloid film. With acetone, we made a paste from the celluloid films and used it to join several layers of canvas together. With four or five layers, we had a sheet, which we pressed lightly and let dry. Once a sheet became dry and hard, it was ready to cut for soles. The only problem with our invention was the heavy fumes it produced. I prepared the paste-and-canvas sheets in the morning and went skiing or hiking in the afternoon to get some fresh air.

⁓

On March 19, 1944, the German armed forces occupied Hungary. Miklós Horthy, the Regent of the Kingdom of Hungary, had not fully cooperated with the Nazi German government, and the occupation was the consequence. The fifth column – German sympathizers, the *Schwaben* (Hungarian citizens of German origin), and Hungarian fascists – were ready to help the occupation forces. Under the new and ongoing anti-Jewish laws, the Hungarian police force began to do everything possible to push the Jews out of their businesses or positions, and they also expropriated their apartments for gentile Hungarian citizens.

During this time, I became engaged to Ibolya, hoping that she would not be deported to a women's forced labour camp. Unfortunately, our engagement did not help either of us. Eventually, she received a notice to report to a collection place, where thousands of Jewish girls and women were forced to gather, including married ones. Although Ibolya's mother had been strict, always watching over us, never leaving us alone in the apartment or giving us much chance to kiss each other, she told Ibolya that had she become pregnant, perhaps she could have stayed at home.

In April 1944, posters and notices in all the newspapers stated that all Jewish men eighteen years and over must report to one of the forced labour camps with only one piece of luggage. Those who ignored the order would be rounded up by the military police and arrested. I was on duty at the fire station when I received my notice to report. The chief of the fire department took my notice and told me that I had to stay with them. He said that my job was more important than enlisting in a good-for-nothing camp. Ten days later, I received another notice. Still I did not respond. Four days later, on May 7, 1944, I was on duty again when armed military police officers came looking for me. I asked them to call my chief. The police officers ordered me to follow them, but my superior advised me to stay put. He told them they needed me in the department. There was a lot of yelling until one of the police officers took out his gun and pointed it at me. I had no choice but to go with them. They escorted me to my home.

Interestingly, they were friendly and joked about my importance to the country. They mused that the Jews had controlled not only Hungary but also the whole world. They said that this was no longer so, because the great Hitler and the faithful Hungarians – "the true Aryan people" – had taken over the reins and now dictated their terms to the Jews. Then they took away my citizenship documents and ordered me to report the next morning to an assembly point on a field outside the city.

At the assembly area, other Jewish men and I were dispatched to one of the labour camps, which was on Lehel Street. This camp supplied several army units with food, tools and firewood. Lieutenant Ujvary, who in civilian life was a teacher, was first in command. This officer happened to be mild-mannered and was not a Nazi sympathizer. We got along with him, even though he slyly kept our meagre weekly pay (one dollar each) for himself. We did not complain about this, as most of us had brought some money from home, just in case.

Working conditions deteriorated when, a little while later, Lieutenant Wiesner became our first commanding officer and Ujvary became second lieutenant. Wiesner was a husky man who dressed in full uniform with a white armband indicating that he, his father or his grandfather had been a Jew but had converted to Christianity. He was a bully who yelled all the time and found extra work for us. He wanted to show that he was a better Hungarian than the best of the "real" Aryan people. Hitting and kicking us for fun and without any provocation were his contributions to the war effort.

Our unit was divided into four sections, each comprised of about one hundred people led by a captain. Our captain, by the name of Beer, also wore a white armband. He was even meaner than Wiesner. He was so sadistic that, right after liberation, one of the Jewish men he had terrorized shot him dead.

Upon our arrival, our sergeant asked for a shoemaker to make and repair boots and shoes, a tailor, a general repairman and a medic. I volunteered as a shoemaker. A man named George Deutch volunteered as a medic, since he had finished the first year of medical school. To get a break from the camp, he made a lot of house calls, which were not exactly of a medical nature; he stayed in basements where windows opened onto back streets, so he could escape if the Nazis showed up.

Lieutenant Ujvary never questioned my knowledge of boot repair – although it was quite different from making and repairing shoes, which is what I had experience in. Since there were no tools, materials or any of the necessary equipment, I asked Ujvary for a pass, which he gave me, to go home to pick up materials and tools for the boot repair. At home, I gathered food from our kitchen and materials from our factory to bring to the camp. After this, I often, intentionally, would find one of the labourers' boots beyond repair, which gave him the chance to go home and get another pair of boots. He would receive a pass for a few days for this.

I noticed that Lieutenant Ujvary had an old pair of riding boots, and I offered to make a brand new pair for him at no cost, which he gladly accepted. I requested a pass on three occasions to go home for materials. I took the best materials for boots and gave them to a real bootmaker. He took the measurements I gave him and made an excellent pair of boots. Since he kept the material that was left over, I didn't have to pay him anything. The boots pleased Lieutenant Ujvary, and I developed a good relationship with him.

We worked at the camp for approximately three months and then moved to a new location, which had previously been a tavern. Four weeks later, the Germans took over the place, and in September, we moved to Gömb Street into a building that had formerly been a school. We set up shop and kept busy. The other units had to work in different places, digging out people and valuables after air raids or bombings and assisting fire and rescue units. The work for these units was not easy and quite dangerous. Sometimes the walls collapsed or the floors caved in.

My job repairing shoes and boots was easy enough, but when everyone was needed on the field, I had to join my comrades. Once, I worked in a unit whose task was to dig out all the paintings, linen and fine dishes from a high-ranking officer's house that had been directly hit during a bombardment.

Every day at noon, the camp's kitchen staff had to deliver food to the units that were working far away from the camp. The food was carried in three barrels: one for the soup, one for the main dish, which consisted of potatoes and some meat, and one for chicory coffee. One day, I asked Ujvary for permission to help deliver the food, and he agreed. First, we went to my house and gave plenty of food to my mother and sister. My family needed the extra food, and this supplement could last for a whole week. The other delivery guys left me to visit with my family. Later they came back for me, and we returned to the camp, where I finished the daily shoe repairs.

I had completed this trip on four different occasions when one day, during my visit at home, four military police officers entered our building. They were looking for people who had left their units illegally and were hiding. Our main gate was locked all the time, and only the superintendent had the key to it.

As soon as the police came in, the superintendent's wife told me to hide in the attic, above the third floor. She opened the lock for me. I heard a lot of noise downstairs. They were searching every floor, and it sounded as if they had found people hidden in several apartments.

As I heard them order the superintendent to open the attic door, I crawled under a wood-plank walkway. They walked over me, but fortunately did not see me. It was so dusty from the chimney's soot that they left the attic shortly.

A few minutes later, my food delivery unit returned to pick me up. Everybody was calling my name, and the officer in charge was really mad that they were wasting so much time looking for me. He foresaw problems in returning late to the camp. Finally, I made my way down and reported to the officer in true military fashion. He asked me if I had been hiding in the chimney. I replied no, otherwise I would be black from soot. All the men started to laugh. The officer told me to take a look at my reflection in a nearby window. I did and saw that my face was, indeed, black and covered in soot.

Because of this dangerous episode and much tighter camp security in general, I was no longer able to join the food delivery group. More inspectors came to check attendance at the camp. As the Red Army crossed the Hungarian border and rapidly advanced, there was heavy fighting. With the increase in air raids, our work became harder; cleanup and rescue operations took up most of our time.

At the end of September 1944, about one hundred young Jewish men, aged eighteen to twenty, joined us from some units that had completed their work on assigned tasks. In the new group was Tibor, my sister's boyfriend. This coddled "mama's boy" had to select his socks and shirts by himself for the first time in his life. Since physical work was difficult for him, I did my best to help him. I also met George Glass, a friendly, hard-working guy. Although George was in one of the work units, he often managed to leave and go home to see Baba, his wife. This caused trouble for him and the whole unit. George happened to be at home in mid-October when Miklós Horthy, the Regent of Hungary, made his declaration of intent to make peace with the Allied forces, including the Soviet Union. That same day, the fascist Arrow Cross Party, with the support of the Nazi regime, seized power in a coup. Instead of returning to his unit, George went into hiding.

Everything was in chaos. Lieutenant Ujvary called me into his office and said, "My boy, I am sorry to say that you have to pack your repair shop into boxes – everything. The unit is going far away. If you have some plans in your head, talk to Private Jozsi Denes, a gypsy soldier, and have some money ready. I wish you good luck, and if we survive this unfortunate and terrible war, we will celebrate together. What I have told you is confidential." I shook his hand and replied, "Thank you very much, and I wish you good luck as well. You have been a real gentleman. Take care, and God bless you."

I understood what Ujvary meant. I told Tibor and eight other close friends that I was planning an escape because, in view of the takeover of the government, the unit would almost certainly soon be forced to go to Germany to work for the war effort, and I asked them to join me. I told them we would have to pay somebody a bribe to look the other way while we escaped. We managed to put together some money that our families had given us.

The next evening, I asked Jozsi, the guard, to come to the repair shop so I could adjust the heels on his boots. I revealed our plan to him and asked for his cooperation. I gave him the money we had collected, an amount he was content with. According to our plan, he would be on duty during the morning at the side entrance, a fence of wood planks. He said he would intentionally "look the other way" for ten minutes. This would be sufficient time for the ten of us to escape by moving away a loose plank.

Everything was set. I put my repair equipment into boxes and left all my clothes hanging from the nails. At 5:00 the next morning, we left the room quietly. Jozsi was there, as he had said he would be. I was the last one to go through the fence. One of my legs was outside the fence when a German army unit, made up of about fifty soldiers, passed by. I pretended I was repairing the broken fence. The soldiers glanced at me but did not stop. In the last seconds of the ten-minute reprieve, I made it outside. What a close call!

I removed the yellow band from my arm and bid farewell to my friends. With money in hand, I boarded the first streetcar that came by. Luckily, it was almost empty and the elderly conductor did not seem to care who I was.

When I came back to Budapest after the war, I was saddened to learn that none of the friends with whom I had escaped survived the war.

Homecoming without a Home

On October 16, 1944, I arrived to a home full of strangers. Because the bombardments had damaged so many apartment buildings, residents had been relocated to share living space in those apartments or houses that had only a few occupants. Since strangers were present, I greeted my mother and sister not like a son or brother but just as an acquaintance. My mother and sister were preparing to go away to a farm, with the help of a former factory worker, under the new identities of refugees from Kisvárda. I said, "See you, Ilonka," to my mother and, "See you, Borka," to my sister. They replied, "Take care, Laci." I didn't see my mother again until fifteen years later and my sister, who was sixteen years old at that time, until twenty-four years later.

After that strange goodbye, I felt heartbroken. I went to see my gentile friend Leslie Toth, the gentleman who had introduced me to the dance studio. He was home with his girlfriend and, luckily, wanted to help me. He gave me his own official army document, which stated that Leslie Toth had been released from duty because of chronic arthritis and was therefore unfit to serve.

He also gave me the address of a religious Jew who was selling birth certificates. These certificates were original, blank documents with official stamps and signatures on them. Even the serial numbers were real. I asked him for one, but his price was US$100, which I did not have. Knowing that my life was in his hands, I tried desperately to convince him to give me a birth certificate. After his repeated refusals, I lost my temper and hit him, hard. I told him that when the Germans captured him, they would take away all his money, jewellery and documents. That seemed to do the trick, and he gave me the certificate. I returned to my friend Leslie, and his girlfriend filled out the form. My name was now Leslie Toth, my mother's name Ilona (her real name), father's name unknown. The certificate looked real – used and a little dirty. By assuming a new identity, I was able to cover up my past. My documents stated that I was Leslie Toth, but in my mind, I was still a Jew.

Leslie then took my photo from my army documents and went to a bakery that made bread mostly for the army but also for the public. Leslie asked the owner, who was his relative, to give me an official document stating that I worked in the bakery as an employee for the war effort. The owner inserted my photo in a document, put the official stamp on it and signed it.

I spent a couple of weeks with Leslie and his girlfriend. It was then time for his girlfriend to go back to her apartment and to her work as a clerk in Buda in a Gestapo office. By then, the beginning of November, the Margit Bridge between Pest and Buda had been damaged in an explosion, and the army had built a temporary bridge. Everybody who wanted to cross it had to present a pass and give a reason for crossing. Armed soldiers were stationed at two checkpoints on each side.

Leslie approached one checkpoint and showed his identification papers. His girlfriend and I went to the other one, so as not to have two Leslie Toths crossing from the same checkpoint. I was afraid that the guards would read my name and his out loud, which would have caused us more than a bit of a problem. However, Leslie's girlfriend said I was her boyfriend, and all went smoothly.

She had a nice, one-bedroom apartment one block away from the Gestapo building. This was not very reassuring for me. We all stayed together a short while longer, and then decided it would be safer to separate. Leslie and his girlfriend went to a large farm south of Budapest, and I had no choice but to risk my life and walk back to the Pest side of the city. Luckily, once again, I didn't encounter any problems. For a few days, I hid in a bombed-out building and ate whatever I was able to find. Then I felt ready to face the dangers ahead.

It was tricky to avoid the police raids and the Arrow Cross fascists who had taken over the government; they were notorious for murdering any Jews they caught. I had to take a chance and go to the municipal government office to apply for an apartment or a room. I took my place at the end of a long line of people waiting to go into the office on Rákóczi Avenue. One hour later, I saw a group of police officers stopping everybody for identification. Sensing trouble, even though I had my false identification papers, I slowly walked away. In the afternoon when I returned, I heard that the police had arrested many. This time, I did not have any problems; I told the government officials my old home had been bombed and that I needed a new place to live. They gave me a room in a three-bedroom apartment on Király Street.

A waitress who worked in a hotel restaurant occupied one room. I had to have a roommate; he was a fifteen-year-old who I learned was also Jewish. The third room was too damaged to be inhabited, but in the closet I found a pair of high-laced boots resembling those used by the Arrow Cross, and a wide belt, which I used on the outside of my coat. I also grew a moustache. All these things gave me enough confidence to act the part of Leslie Toth.

A week later, officers came from the fire department and called everybody downstairs into the courtyard for a tenants' meeting. They informed us that every building had to have a volunteer air-raid captain who would be in charge of sending people to the shelter during air raids, fighting small fires and organizing small rescue operations. When I told them about my firefighting experience, they gave me the job. They supplied me with a firefighter's helmet, heavy belt, axe, rope and flashlight. Was I ever happy, and official to boot!

The Arrow Cross guards came almost daily to search for Jews who were hiding or for regular soldiers who had left their units to avoid going to the front, where they could be killed. I always gave the guards a proper, official salutation and reported for duty. I escorted them to different parts of the building, avoiding places where I knew some Jews were hiding. They found a few Hungarian and even German soldiers. There were posters all over the city warning soldiers in hiding to return to their units or report to the nearest one. I learned later that my old friend George Glass did just that, but brought a few items of civilian clothes with him. When he learned that the unit was going to travel to Austria or Germany a few days later, he snuck out once again and went into hiding.

One late Sunday afternoon in November, while I was on my way to exchange a woman's scarf I had found for bread, an Arrow Cross guard stopped me and, without asking for any documents, escorted me to Nagykörút (Grand Boulevard), a major road in the city, rounding up others along the way. We were made to face the storefronts, which were all shuttered, and the guards began shooting their captives at random. I collapsed when the shooting started, and a wounded girl fell upon me. In that instant, the air-raid sirens sounded and the guards stopped shooting and ran away as fast as they could. Looking around, I saw only the dead. I pushed away the bodies and ran to the nearest apartment building. It was empty – all the residents must have been in the bomb shelter – so I entered an apartment. Luckily, I found some men's clothing to change into from my blood-soaked coat. Avoiding the patrols and the falling bombs, I went home to my Király Street room, put on my firefighter's helmet and avoided people, so as not to reveal my terrified state of mind. Considering how narrowly I had escaped death, it felt as if I was born a second time.

Going out to buy or exchange items for food continued to be risky, but it had to be done. One day, I took a bedsheet and a blanket and went to see a woman who had worked in my family's factory some time before. She gave me a small bag of beans and a skinny duck in exchange. For more than a week, my roommate and I ate duck and beans. Another time, I exchanged three pairs of shoes for a kilo of flour and ten potatoes.

One late afternoon, I heard that the corner store had obtained sugar and salt. On my way there, I was stopped by armed Arrow Cross guards, who demanded to see my ID papers. The older one said my papers were acceptable, but the younger one, who was about seventeen, said they were not. He insisted on taking me to their headquarters at 60 Andrássy Avenue. Everone knew that people were interrogated, tortured and killed there. I lost all hope; I believed I would die before experiencing happiness, having my own family or living a normal life.

As we passed the small park between Király Street and Andrássy Avenue, I heard some loud noise. Then somebody pushed me in the back and yelled, "Run! Run fast!" I did, but before I turned the corner, I glanced back. The younger soldier lay on the sidewalk bleeding profusely, and the older one, who had shot him, was running away. Then I remembered having seen the older guard somewhere else, and I realized that he was a Jew and must have been passing as a non-Jew in the fascist unit. I hope he survived the war. He saved my life. I think of this fortuitous escape as being born a third time.

~

Soon after this incident, I heard about Raoul Wallenberg, the Swedish diplomat who was giving protective visas called *Schutzpässe* to Jews to save them from deportation out of the country or to the newly established Budapest ghetto. One morning I went to the Swedish legation, located in a beautiful villa, and joined a long, slow-moving line. By about 2:00 p.m., I was among the group about to go inside the gate next when a large Arrow Cross unit passed by. I ran away just as some of those waiting were captured and taken away. The next day I tried again, but yet again the Arrow Cross came by and began to surround the villa. I was unable to obtain a *Schutzpass*.

By December 1944, the Arrow Cross raids and ID checks had become relentless. I constantly worried that the Arrow Cross would not accept my false ID and would discover I was Jewish and shoot me on the spot. So I found a way to sneak into the Budapest ghetto, which I considered safer, and to our old home, the shoe factory. Using leftover material and our tools, I started to repair boots and shoes, which I planned to trade for food.

That December, the Arrow Cross changed the colour of the Danube River from blue to red. The river runs from the Black Forest in Germany through the middle of Vienna and divides Hungary's capital into two parts, Buda and Pest. "The Blue Danube," composed by Johann Strauss ii, is one of the most beautiful waltz melodies, and the Viennese waltz is my favourite dance. The Arrow Cross committed the most heinous crimes along the banks of this beautiful river – I was horrified to find out that when the Arrow Cross captured Jews on the streets or in their homes, they escorted them to the Danube. There, they made the Jews line up and, without hesitation, shot them. Countless bodies floated down the blood-stained river.

I wonder what these men thought of their actions years later and whether they had regrets. At the time, I wished that they and their leaders would rot in jail for a very long time. Yet I now know that many of them later found refuge in other countries, including Canada, and lived or are living normal lives, having never been punished for their crimes.

Going East

By the end of December 1944, the siege of Budapest had begun. The liberators were finally changing the direction of the wind, but they came too late. Thousands of innocent people had already been blown away. The Hungarians and the Germans did not declare Budapest to be an "open city," which would have meant surrendering to the advancing Red Army and, ultimately, less destruction and loss of life. Consequently, bitter fighting took place, street to street.

In the beginning of January, Hungarian soldiers were rounding up Jews, mostly men, in the ghetto almost every day. I decided that it would be best to go back out to the apartment on Király Street. I found a tunnel in the basement of one of the buildings on Kisdiófa Street and was able to sneak out without anybody stopping me. It seemed safer to be on the outside once again.

The building in which I was hiding, on the corner of Király Street, was eight storeys high. From my window, which faced a small side street, I was able to see the defending Nazis one day and the Red Army offensive the next. This see-saw battle went on for weeks until January 17, 1945, when the Red Army broke through and advanced to the centre of the city.

We greeted the first Red Army unit with happy tears in our eyes. The commanding officer understood a little Hungarian. After I informed him of the German and Hungarian soldiers hiding in the

building in civilian clothing, he had the building searched and captured some of them. He also arranged to have plenty of food brought
to all the hungry people. For the first time, I went to sleep in the
bomb shelter without fear that somebody would take me away. I was
a free man, able to start a new life, and I dreamt of my future.

The next morning, a new unit, made up of tall, heavy-set, tired
Ukrainian soldiers, arrived. The first soldier took away my official
documents, the second took my flashlight and the third told me and
some other men to follow him. He led us from our basement to another, where there were sixty to seventy people. The soldiers there
searched us and took away knives, documents if people still had any,
and even family photos. Then a Hungarian translator told us about
the newly established Hungarian government in the city of Debrecen.
This government had representatives not far from Budapest, and all
of us were to go there to receive new documents. We eagerly followed
the leading army officer, not noticing that armed soldiers surrounded
us. By late evening we had arrived at a small house, which was our
accommodation for the night. We hadn't received food or anything to
drink all day. The Jewish boy who had been my roommate on Király
Street was also there.

In the early morning, a heavy Ukrainian soldier came in and
asked, "Yid? Yevrey?" He was asking who was Jewish. My young
friend wanted to stand up, but I forced him to sit and be quiet. I studied the face of this soldier, and did not find it friendly. One man stood
up in the back. The soldier signalled to the man to follow him. A few
minutes later he was dead, killed by this soldier. These Ukrainians
hated the Jews as much as the Nazis did.

With foot and mounted soldiers around us, we walked to Gödöllő,
about thirty kilometres northeast of Budapest. Some men who tried
to escape were shot on the spot. Once we reached the Hungarian Agricultural University in Gödöllő, we received a slice of black bread
and a cup of liquid that they called coffee. The university had two
large and many smaller buildings, barbed wire all around and numer-

ous armed guards, some with dogs, to keep more than ten thousand people inside; we were told that this was a camp for prisoners of war, P O W s. With such tight security, nobody could escape. I saw only one person released. I did not even think about escaping. I gave up on my future, and complete lethargy came over me. I lost the will to live.

Moving around the camp, I found Ibolya's brother, Andrew. He was so happy to see me and from then on, he was always by my side. He asked me to look after him. I didn't tell him that I couldn't even look after myself. Twice a day, we were given a bowl of soup and a slice of black bread. There was no facility to take a shower, and the latrines were holes in the ground with a few wooden planks spread across on which we had to balance. Our only occupation was getting rid of lice on our bodies and finding a small spot where we could lie down, stretch out and be able to have a few hours of sleep. Every day, we were told the new Hungarian government in Debrecen would issue ID cards. With these cards, we would be free to go home. This was a lie to keep us all under control.

Weeks later, a Soviet delegation came to the camp. The delegation included women who were medically trained doctors' assistants and several officers from the N K V D, the Soviet intelligence service. We had to line up, twenty to thirty at a time, completely naked. They checked our eyes for trachoma, an infectious disease; pinched our buttocks to check our muscle mass and strength; grabbed our testicles to see if we had any venereal diseases; and looked into our mouths. They treated us as if we were horses at an auction, a truly humiliating experience. A few prisoners were rejected and left the camp within the hour. I was declared *horosho*, okay, meaning I was free of any sickness and in decent shape. With the others, I was led to a barrack, where we each received plain clothing, a dish, a spoon, a cup and a slice of bread.

The next morning, we started to march to the city of Cegléd, about seventy kilometres southeast of Budapest. There were five thousand P O W s in our unit, including Ibolya's brother, Andrew. Along the way, the guards kept telling us, "Pyat-pyat," meaning we had to march five abreast. This made it easier for them to count us. Sometimes when they counted more than five thousand, they let the extra prisoners go free; other times, the guards took local civilians to replace missing prisoners.

The guards hit us often with two-metre-long sticks and told us we were fascist pigs and killers and that if it was up to them, they would kill everybody immediately. It gave me some degree of satisfaction seeing the German and Hungarian prisoners treated this way, but I was treated this way, too. Such a fine way to freedom!

By late evening, we were assigned to four large barns, with heavy security around us. Supper consisted of only two slices of bread. After we had slept a short time, the guards started to yell orders to go outside, wait for the head count and get ready to go. In one barn, some people were too sick or too tired to move fast or move at all. The guards started to shoot from the main floor up to the ceiling, not caring whether there were people in the upper section of the barn. They killed one man instantly and injured others slightly. The order of the day was marching again, without food or drink. The head counting and the beatings resumed. The next night there were not enough barns to accommodate five thousand people. Some people, including Andrew and me, slept inside a school, but most of the prisoners slept outside on the ground.

The daily five-abreast march was not the worst part. Thirst was. We hadn't had anything to drink since leaving Gödöllő. On the side of the road, in the ditches, melted snow was running. It was tempting, but I warned everybody not to drink it. Those who did ended up with dysentery. I learned that some of them died in the camp a few days later.

By late afternoon, we arrived at a camp in the city of Cegléd. This was a real POW camp – well organized and fenced in with three rows of barbed wire. In our new barracks, three tiers of bunk beds, each with straw and a worn-out blanket, were waiting for us. How happy we were to receive our first food ration and the black water they called chicory "coffee." The next day, we got some sorely needed clothing. It was winter, and cold. Some of us were given used Soviet army coats, which made it difficult to differentiate between captors and captives. One early morning, a young man wearing an army coat decided to escape. Even though people told him it was hopeless, he started to climb over the fence in the dark. With a piece of rug protecting his hands, he made it over the first two fences, but as he was climbing the third fence, a guard spotted him and yelled, "Stoj!" (Stop!) Either the young man didn't understand the order or he didn't care to stop. The guard shot him dead.

I later learned that my mother had looked for me in Budapest and Cegléd, asking around as to whether people had seen me. Somebody told her that I was the one who had been killed by a guard while trying to escape. With the alleged loss of my father and the misleading news about my death, she had no reason to remain in Hungary. The Red Cross arranged for my mother and sister to go to a refugee camp in Germany.

Ten days after we arrived at the POW camp, those in charge asked for volunteers to bring some empty wooden barrels into the camp. I volunteered and went with the group to the marmalade factory in Cegléd. The factory was empty except for a lot of used barrels without covers. As we rolled the barrels to the camp, we could see a thin layer of leftover marmalade on the bottom. On the way, we were able to scoop some out and eat it. It was old and stale, but it provided some sustenance.

There was a small guy with a big hat who was not able to roll and eat at the same time. As he was leaning into a barrel, one of the guards pushed him inside as a joke. We could see only his legs, but had to keep on rolling the barrel, with him inside. Later, when Red Cross representatives came into the camp, they gathered all the people who were sixteen years and under and transported them to Debrecen. That small guy was among those lucky few who were freed.

On March 2, 1945, a large group of us was taken to the railroad siding, where a cattle train stood ready to go. Sixty people were assigned to one car, which was equipped with straw, blankets, an empty pail for a toilet and one of those barrels, which had been cut in half and fitted with wire handles. The half-barrel served as a container to pick up our food twice a day. High up was a little barred window. We lived in this "hotel" for the next ten days as the train moved along. Food – soup, a slice of bread and a spoonful of sugar – was provided when the train stopped in the morning and evening; the train stopped often during the day because the railroad lines were busy transporting supplies and soldiers to the front. During these stops, we emptied our toilet pail. Existence in this one-room compartment was extremely difficult. Quarrelling, and even some physical fighting, occurred daily.

At each stop, we questioned people about our whereabouts through our little window. On one such occasion, somebody told us that we were in Romania. The guards didn't let anybody too close to the train. At one stop, locals called out some names, hoping that missing relatives and friends were on the train with us.

After ten days of travelling, the train stopped and the guards opened the doors. It was difficult to walk again. Everybody was miserable, unshaven, unwashed and smelly. We saw oil wells, refineries and gasoline or crude oil tanks. A sign read "Ploieşti." Since the city of Ploieşti had the largest refinery in Romania, it had been a major supplier for the German and Italian armies. Romania had been allied with Germany during the war, and Germany had used all its resources and workforce.

The POW camp, on the outskirts of Ploieşti, had been an army camp before and during the war. When the Romanian government severed its relationship with Germany, it had to empty all military camps. The camp was well organized: on each bed in the barracks was a blanket, a small but clean towel and some eating utensils. Within a short time, we were in the showers and our clothes went through a disinfection process. Before we received our clean, lice-free clothing, another group of POWs shaved us from top to bottom. Their razors were neither the latest model nor the sharpest ones. A little blood here or there didn't matter; we were clean.

You have to experience a journey such as the one we had taken to truly appreciate a shower, a bloody shave and a meal of potato soup, cooked barley with some traces of meat, a piece of black bread and coffee with a spoonful of white sugar. These were luxuries to us. We then took our place in the assigned barracks. One added luxury: we were able to stretch out to sleep.

The camp's population included different nationalities: French, Belgian, Romanian, Yugoslavian and Greek. I didn't understand why any of us were here, though maybe some had fought alongside the Nazis. We were in the main camp, which was used as a collection point – after organizing the group into units of fifty people, the Soviet officers sent each unit out of the main camp. To my great surprise, I found myself placed with Andrew and thirty other Jews. Among them were David, a captain in the Polish army who had taken part in the 1944 Warsaw uprising, and Jani, a lieutenant in the Yugoslavian army who had fought with Josip Broz Tito in the resistance group. He was still in uniform. Although David and Jani spoke Slavic languages and showed their ID papers to the Red Army when they were "liberated," the Red Army's orders were to trust no one and to question the authenticity of any document.

One of the men in my unit was Jozsi (Joseph) Kohn, who had come back to Budapest from a concentration camp with an official release paper. He was just three blocks from his home when a Soviet soldier ordered him to join a small group of people for a few hours of work. Then the Soviets told the workers the same thing I had been told – to go to an office to receive new Hungarian documents before they went home. This trick, which was used to get people to a POW camp, was a story repeated thousands of times by people in the POW camps. Many of the people the Soviets now treated as POWs had survived the Nazi labour and concentration camps, yet the liberation forces took them to yet another camp. We were in the wrong place at the wrong time.

Earlier, while the train that was taking us to Romania was being loaded with water and coal in Debrecen, a tall, handsome guy who looked a few years older than me stood on the platform waiting for a passenger train. After the officers did a head count and came up one man short, they grabbed this man and put him in one of the cattle cars. His name was Leslie Frankel and he explained that he had been with the partisans, had an official document from the new Hungarian government and was working in the special police force to capture Nazis in hiding. After the war, some Jewish ex-forced labourers joined the new police and armed forces to search for war criminals. Although Leslie spoke Russian quite well and the Red Army officer repeatedly said, "Horosho" (Good), Leslie, who had been on that platform awaiting his girlfriend, was forced to take the place of the missing body in the transport and come with us.

On March 20, 1945, we once again were made to board the cattle cars of a long train. With fifty people in one boxcar, we had more space than in our previous train ride. The conditions were also better: there were blankets and better food, and we had bigger windows, although they had metal rods across them. The officers also distributed *machorka* (tobacco), but since I did not smoke, I exchanged mine for a half-spoon of sugar.

Ten days later, after everyone in the car had shared their heartbreaking stories, we arrived in the village of Kadievka in Eastern Ukraine, the heart of the coal quarry district called Donetsk. On the way to the camp, we did not see a single undamaged house or barn. The German army had destroyed everything and taken every movable piece of furniture, farm animal and item of food. Only a few trees were standing – the rest had been cut down for firewood or for use in the repair of transportation equipment. Once again, I felt no hope for my future.

There were thirty-two Jews in our group. The rest of the men there were hardcore German Nazis who had continued fighting even after the Red Army had overtaken the terrain. David, our spokesperson, asked a Soviet officer for a meeting with the camp's commanding officer. He wanted to inform the officer that we had been the victims of the Nazis and that treating us as POWs was a grave mistake. The commanding officer agreed to see us, but first we had to go through a disinfection procedure required of all prisoners entering a camp. This meant taking off all our clothes and setting aside any piece of paper or other flammable material, as well as combs, which could harbour lice. After we hung up our clothes on metal hooks, the racks of clothes, which were on rollers, were pushed into another room. This room was like an oven, heating up to a high temperature to kill all the lice and any other bugs in the clothes. The clothes often caught fire. Then we were led to a room and each given a piece of soap, three litres of hot water and a small towel. Again, we received a complete shaving from top to bottom. We were then given our hot, bug-free clothes and were ready to enter the camp.

The commanding officer met us in a separate building. He was a lieutenant-general in the Red Army, with many decorations on his uniform. He greeted us in a friendly fashion and asked which of us was David and who would translate our discussion. David introduced himself as a captain in the Polish army. The commanding officer told us that he was Jewish, too, and wanted to hear all our stories. First, the Slavic-speaking people told their short stories, and then the Hungarians, with the aid of a translator, told theirs. The officer had tears running down his face and said, "I will take care of you like nobody else! You were forced to work for the Germans and to help the Germans fight the war. Now, here you are liberated; you need no longer fear for your life. You will have a future. Now it is time to do some work for the Soviet Union to help her to recover from her terrible losses."

We left to pick up our meal, full of hope that we would go home soon. Our new living quarters were a large barn with upper and lower bunk beds, each with a straw-filled mattress and pillow, one large blanket, a large towel and a piece of soap. A German P O W, I think his name was Fritz, came in and introduced himself as the head of the barrack. He was to keep the personnel list and assign us to a working station. He reported to the Soviet camp commander, but as he read out a long list of dos and don'ts for the camp, it felt as if we were once again under German command, rules and regulations, once again enduring German language and German hatred.

According to international humanitarian law, prisoners of war must be supplied with food, clothing and health care. A P O W can volunteer for work, but can also refuse to work. We were quarantined for twenty-one days so the officers could ensure we were free of bugs and any potentially contagious sickness. The quarantine period also allowed us to gain strength and recover from illness.

During our quarantine, the Red Cross handed out three postcards to each person, so that we could write to family members or friends. I wrote to my mother at Klauzál Square, to Ibolya's parents and to my uncle Erno. We couldn't write places, names or about our work, so I wrote, "I have my brother-in-law with me." Andrew did the same.

In the Soviet Union, offices, factories and armed forces units had a secretary of the Communist Party and an officer from the N K V D. They acted as overseers, and the N K V D officer saw every production report and questioned everybody. He constructed a web of information along with some misinformation. In our camp, the N K V D officer was Jewish and his name was Captain Shumacher. He was a tall, slim, fast-moving and fast-thinking man, with a constant smile plastered on his face. His smile was his best tool for worming his way into people's confidence.

During our quarantine, we all had to fill in a four-page questionnaire, written in Russian. With the help of a translator, we answered every single question regarding our education, parents, places of work and positions. A full page of questions related to the period of the war. The questions were purposely tricky; if you lied in one answer, your next answer could easily contradict the previous one.

One of the questions was, "What did you do in 1943 month by month?" I answered that I had worked in the Tatra Shoe Factory. I did not say that my family was the owner. The NKVD officer studied every line carefully. He had a system to find out if someone had lied. In the middle of the night, he would call an individual into his office and ask only a few questions. A few days later, he would ask the same questions, never commenting on the answers he had received. He was able to catch a number of Germans with a bloody past. I saw several people with packed bags taken away from the camp. I learned that they were taken to Moscow to the NVKD headquarters for further interrogation. I also heard that one of the German POWs who had been an SS-*Oberscharführer*, a high rank in the SS, stole a single piece of potato and that another German, who had been in the Wehrmacht, the regular army, reported this to the NVKD officer. The next day, the ex-SS was escorted out of the camp to an army jail and sentenced to ten years of hard labour. The theft of the piece of potato was just an excuse to punish an SS officer.

One night around 2:00 a.m., somebody woke me and told me to report to the NKVD officer. He greeted me with a smile and, with the help of a translator, asked only one question: "What did you do in June of 1943?" I told him I was with the volunteer fire department. He said thanks and let me go back to sleep. A few days later, he again summoned me, at about 3:00 a.m., and asked the same question. I gave him the same answer. Five minutes of silence followed, during which I started to worry. He then asked me if I was a real Jew. I said yes. He asked, "Why did you lie on the questionnaire? Were you a worker in a factory or a firefighter?" Slowly, I explained to him that I both volunteered at the fire department and worked at the factory, but in different shifts. He asked a few more questions and told me that he was pleased to find out that I was an innocent survivor of the war who was, unfortunately, in the POW camp among German soldiers. He said there were more than one hundred war criminals in the camp and it would only be a matter of time before they were identified. He asked me to keep my ears open and report anything I thought would help him to catch these people. I slept very well after my final interrogation by Captain Shumacher.

One day before the quarantine was over, our barracks head, Fritz, came and told me and the thirty-one other Jews to assemble outside the barracks. We jumped for joy and ignored the nasty antisemitic remarks made by the German POWs. We thought that surely we were going home then, thanks to the commanding officer. Instead, four armed guards escorted us on a march of more than one hour to an open-pit limestone quarry. There, some locals gave us hammers, metal wedges, pickaxes, shovels and a primitive stone carrier, which looked like a short stretcher. They gave us brief instructions about what to do and then left. Our job was to cut, hammer and slice the limestone from the bedrock, carry it up to the open field and pile it in cubic metres. From the limestone, a group of locals constructed a chimney shaped like a tall tower and burned it. From the white ash left over, white paint for the houses being built in the town would be made. Everything in the area had been destroyed in the war and the Soviet government's priority was to rebuild.

We had to produce a daily minimum quota: twelve cubic metres. If we did not produce enough cubic metres of stone, then the camp kitchen withheld one slice of bread from each person in the group the following day. Due to our limited experience, we didn't produce the quota about half the time.

The quarry became deeper and deeper, making it harder to bring up the heavy load of stones. At first, one "stretcher" was enough to carry the stones, but later two stretchers were needed because the greater distance from the bottom of the pit made it too hard to carry such a heavy load. Fewer and fewer people were able to hammer, chisel and shovel out the stone from the bedrock and into cubic-metre units. At 4:00 p.m., the *nachalnik*, our supervisor, came to measure the amount of limestone; he then wrote a report on our progress to give to the guard to deliver to the German camp officer.

One of my workmates had been a first-year university student in the architecture faculty. He had a good idea about how to make the cubic metres with fewer stones: by piling the stones a certain way, we could leave a lot of empty space inside that wouldn't be visible from the outside. Using this method, we would be able to meet our quota and receive our bread ration every time. One day the *nachalnik* became suspicious and kicked the cubic metre, which collapsed. When he found out the stones amounted to little more than half of a cubic metre, he was furious and he used his whole, rich vocabulary of curse words. For four weeks, we had to do extra work on Saturdays until 1:00 p.m. to compensate the supervisor for the missing production.

I worked down in the pit, hammering wedges into the veins of the rocks. When a slab was loose enough, I pried the piece out with a crowbar. One day, I started singing. During the ten-minute rest period, one of the guards came over and asked me why I was singing so happily. With an interpreter, I told him, "I am alive, not too hungry and fairly healthy, and I hope my bad luck will change for the better." The guard instructed me to take a half-hour break instead of the group's ten-minute break, and during this time, I was to sing a song. He reported to the supervisor that he was one man short and that the quota should be reduced accordingly.

The hard work and the reduced food soon took its toll: we all lost weight and sported bruises and injuries. Andrew, who was not used to hard work, grew extremely weak. He was always complaining, but one morning he was really unable to get out of bed. We took him to the infirmary before we left for work. When we came back, he had a high fever and was in severe pain, but the German doctor on duty said that Andrew was faking sickness. They kept him in the infirmary for days, giving him no medication besides Aspirin. I visited him there twice. The day after my second visit, they transported Andrew to the nearest hospital, where he died a few hours later. He had

had a kidney infection, and without timely treatment, both kidneys stopped working. He was only twenty years old.

I felt both sad and angry. I wondered what I would say to Andrew's parents. How could I explain to them that I had been unable to take better care of him? Why were the Jewish prisoners assigned to hard and dangerous work a day before our quarantine lapsed while the German prisoners were assigned to lighter work? The German prisoners had been taken to a construction site after the full length of quarantine. There, they built door and window frames from logs and made bricks and shingles for the new houses. Our "saviour," the Jewish commanding officer, arranged the work assignments to show the Communist Party secretary and the rest of his Soviet comrades that he was a good Soviet citizen and did not favour Jewish P O W s. He had promised to take care of us and told us that our life would not be in danger anymore. He had lied.

The security around the camp and work sites was tight. During the year that I was in this camp, only three people managed to escape: one froze to death in an open field, the locals killed another one and the third escaped in the summer but was captured 150 kilometres away by a mounted army unit. The unit brought him back to the camp, but he died the next day. The officer said he died of a heart attack.

Our camp supplied the labour for a construction company run by the local Soviet government. The construction company, tasked with building houses, had to install water, sewage and electrical systems and coordinate the installation of bricks, shingles and woodwork. At that time, about two hundred houses had been constructed on each street. The goal was to build approximately five thousand one-bedroom homes.

We, the prisoners, worked alongside local Ukrainians and were assigned to different workplaces, which were surrounded by Soviet armed guards who were mostly from another part of Russia. The guards hated the Ukrainians, but mostly they hated the prisoners. Although the local Ukrainians were Soviet citizens, they were not considered trustworthy, because they had collaborated with the Germans during the war. They were required to do six to twelve months of "rehabilitation work." During this period, they received small salaries and could not leave the district without permission. Once their time had been served, they were issued an internal passport, which enabled them to travel or stay on the job with higher salaries.

From time to time, a freight train delivered a large shipment of logs to the company. From it, all the lumber needed for the houses was produced. No timetable governed the arrival of the trains. The freight could arrive in the morning, afternoon or even late evening. The assigned workers had to go to the train and unload it within the shortest time possible. The trains were in short supply and were needed everywhere for the rebuilding of the country.

The logs were used to make wooden floors, doors and window frames. The frames of the houses were also made out of wood. The lumber was first treated in a steam house and then dried. Often, there was not enough time to dry it completely before it was rushed to a construction site. Consequently, the windows would not open or the doors stuck, due to the moisture in the wood frames. The work was dangerous. The logs were large and heavy, and people were injured daily. Sometimes, when a log was not carefully handled, people died.

The workers went for breakfast at 6:00 a.m. and started work at 7:00 a.m. At 10:00 a.m. and 3:00 p.m, there were ten-minute breaks, and the working day was over at 5:00 p.m. After returning to the camp, we ate lunch: a thin soup; a main dish of cabbage, beets or barley; a cup of black coffee and a slice of black bread.

Every evening at 7:00 p.m., the prisoners assembled for a head count. We had to stay put until the guards got the number right, which sometimes took more than an hour. After that, we received our working orders for the next day. This was the time when a barrack could get permission to go to the shower house, when everyone could take a hot shower and get a bloody shave; this was heaven to us.

Then, supper, which was the same type of food as lunch, was served from 8:00 p.m. With this meal, we also got a spoonful of white sugar, a spoonful of *machorka* and a piece of newspaper for cigarette paper.

Since we had begun working at the stone quarry, David, the Polish captain, had often gone to see the NKVD officer. David told him about how the Jewish Soviet commanding officer had given Jewish prisoners the worst possible jobs and the German prisoners the relatively easier work. After we had spent three long months toiling at the quarry, David brought us good news: the NKVD officer had written a compelling report recommending the replacement of the commanding officer with one who would treat the Germans the way they deserved.

A few weeks later, after the evening head count, the other Jewish POWs and I were given new assignments in the wood-processing section of the construction unit. I was to work at the shingle-making site, which supplied raw wood for the door- and window-frame-making unit. My job was to collect the sawdust from underneath the blade of the log-cutting machine; the sawdust would be stored in large containers and used to heat the small kitchen or the barracks in the winter.

The log-cutting machine had five or seven roughly three-metre-long blades. A 150-horsepower electric motor turned these blades vertically, slicing the large logs into wooden planks. The motor drove a leather belt that was about thirty centimetres wide and more than ten metres long and was attached to the log-cutting machine's flywheel.

The sawdust that fell under the machine had to be cleared away constantly. The task was noisy but not hard, and the operation went smoothly unless a log had some large, hard knots. When the blade could not cut one of these knots, it got stuck and the belt fell off the flywheel and slipped away from the motor's pulley. It took a few minutes until the pulley stopped, after which we were able to put the belt back and continue the log cutting. This waiting time until the motor pulley stopped completely reduced our production. Because we all worked on the quota system, the locals, who operated the cutting machine, rushed us to replace the leather belt as fast as we could.

On one unlucky day, the logs were so full of knots that we had already been delayed by one hour. When the machine got stuck yet again and the belt fell off, the log cutters yelled at us to put the belt back on faster. I was supposed to wait until the motor pulley stopped completely, but the yelling kept up and I was afraid that they would send me to another job. The motor was turning slowly when I tried to put the loop of the belt around the pulley. Then the belt got caught around the pulley, spun around it like a roll of paper towel and the end of the belt hit the left side of my face, shattering my eyeglasses. My left ear hurt and began ringing, and I could feel the left side of my face bruising. For a few seconds, I lost consciousness. I was lucky that I didn't have any broken bones. The machine operator was scared and told me to sit down and not work the rest of the day. He put wet towels on my face to reduce the swelling. Without my glasses, and being a little wobbly on my feet, I needed some help to walk back to the camp. In the infirmary, the workers cleaned my face and applied some iodine. Their medical supplies were extremely limited.

My friend Jozsi Kohn found a pair of used eyeglasses for me in the office. They had belonged to a German soldier who had died a few days before. The glasses did not match my prescription, but at least I was able to see better than without them. When I later had an overall checkup at the Jewish Hospital in Budapest, the doctor was surprised that I hadn't sustained any permanent damage to my left eye. My left ear is a different story. Even a light draft, wind or cold causes sharp pain, and I have partial loss of hearing of high-pitched sounds and voices.

The Fourth Time

In August 1945, Japan raised the white flag after being bombed by the United States. It was the official end of World War II, and it was a tremendous relief. I would later learn that six million innocent Jews had perished in the Holocaust. The Soviet Union alone had lost approximately twenty million citizens, mostly young men.

Our camp celebrated the end of the war by doling out double portions of food. The next day, life returned to the old routine, but the working hours grew longer and the quotas increased. More and more logs arrived, usually after the end of the regular workday. This made it a very long day for the people who were assigned to unload the shipment without having had lunch. I had this "pleasure" a few times.

The food did not improve. The cabbage harvest arrived, and while the supply lasted, we had cabbage three times a day. The outside of the cabbage was barely rinsed, and it all went into a soup. Then the beet shipment came. There was the same: almost no washing, as well as no peeling. When our urine turned red, we started worrying that our kidneys were bleeding, but our medic said the natural colour of the beets caused it.

We were always hungry. On Sundays, most of us volunteered to work at harvesting the fields for half a day so we could have a chance to sneak something for ourselves, like onion bulbs or a carrot. We had to eat this food carefully because there were always guards watching us.

I had not eaten any fresh fruit, eggs or meat since the fall of 1944. I became sick from lack of vitamins and developed scurvy from lack of vitamin C. My gums and tongue swelled, and when I ate, the gums bled and my teeth felt loose. Small blisters appeared all over my body. A few days later, these blisters enlarged and yellow pus oozed from them. My calves were so swollen that pushing the skin on them with my finger created a deep dimple, visible even after half an hour. One by one, my teeth fell out. One tooth under the metal dental bridge I had was infected, causing me a lot of pain.

I was admitted to the infirmary, where one of the German health workers, without using any anaesthetic, started to cut out my bridge with an old shoemaker's file in order to extract the inflamed tooth. It was a hard job for him, but imagine how I felt! After more than an hour, the bridge was cut and, using regular pliers, he pulled the tooth out. Now, having both swollen gums and a profusely bleeding cavity, I felt ready to die. The remaining bridge was sharp and interfered with my tongue. One day the bridge fell out; losing this bothersome piece of metal was a real relief.

Unfortunately, I was losing weight quite rapidly. At the same time, more blisters appeared all over my body and my temperature spiked. Since there was no medication anywhere, I had to care for myself. Going to the kitchen or to the latrine became more and more of a struggle. Eventually, I had to use pieces of wood as a crutch. Sometimes my friends helped me walk, but when they were at work during the day, I often chose to give up food and use my remaining energy to go to the latrine. My hair started thinning out and lost its colour, turning completely white.

In the middle of January 1946, at midnight, I crawled back from the latrine thinking, I'm tired of living. There were thousands of dances I wanted to dance, kisses I wished to share and flowers whose fragrance I wanted to inhale, but at that point I was ready for a deadly wind to blow me off the earth and end my misery. I was twenty-one years old.

When I woke up, I was on top of a stretcher, being carried by people from the poorly equipped infirmary into a so-called hospital. I must have been either unconscious or in a semi-coma. I didn't know that a few days prior, the camp had welcomed a real medical doctor. This young, petite woman, just out of medical school, was doing a two-year internship in the camp. After they undressed me, the young doctor (I think her name was Tatjana) took my blood pressure, which was very low, and my temperature, which was sky high. Due to my blurred vision I couldn't see the doctor's face, nor could I answer any of her questions.

I was her first patient and she kept telling me not to worry. One of the helpers went outside to bring in some ice to cool down my body. Then, using tweezers, the doctor removed the top part of every oozing blister. I had more than one hundred of them. Was it ever painful! She soaked a Q-tip in iodine and cleaned the pus out of the open blisters. Although it burned, I was unable to scream. After the first few blisters, I didn't feel anything – I had fainted. When I came to I thought the torture was finally over, but then the doctor took a Q-tip and iodine and rubbed my gums, ignoring the bleeding. I cannot find words to express the agony I felt. I wished that she would stop and let me fade away.

In the evening, my friend Jozsi visited and told me that when he had reported my condition to the doctor a day earlier, the authorities ordered the labourers to dig a grave for me. Because it was winter, the ground was frozen solid, and it took five men all day to finish digging the grave. I told Jozsi I was sorry for the extra work they had had to do and thanked them anyway. When I was eventually discharged from the hospital, my first walk was to see the grave. Three months later, a man suffered a fatal heart attack and was buried there.

For the next week, I received the same treatment every morning. A so-called orderly held my hand while I endured the pain. The doctor had me consume only liquids to start with and then soft food. Using her own money and a piece of soap, she bought a small chicken for me. This was a big deal, because the farmers' market had little to offer. This angel made me chicken soup and spoon-fed me. Even though she cut the meat into tiny pieces, swallowing that first week was painful.

The doctor took some time off from the camp and went to the city hospital to pick up some medical supplies, including some vitamin C pills. The vitamins really helped my recovery. After a while, I was able to walk without any assistance. The fever went down and the smaller blisters started to heal. About ten larger blisters did not heal until I went back to Hungary. Even today, white spots are still visible on my lower legs and chest where the pigmentation died out.

Although the camp's hospital was full and the doctor very busy – many workers had frostbite or broken legs or arms from clearing away logs on the construction site – I felt like her number-one patient. One month passed slowly but with care, nutritious food and a little medication, I noticed that my gums showed signs of healing. The bleeding stopped. I still weighed less than a hundred pounds, but the young doctor had saved my life. I thought of myself as being born a fourth time.

I thanked the doctor constantly. We spent some time together eating in the same room and trying to communicate, me in my broken Ukrainian. The doctor arranged for my transfer to the maintenance unit, where the work was lighter, the food much better and I didn't have to go outside. I was one of the repairmen during the night shift.

A month later, I went looking for the young doctor but she was no longer there. I heard that somebody had reported to the NKVD that she was becoming too friendly with me. She was transferred to another camp on short notice. I never saw her again.

⌒

My new work consisted of repairing clothing, footwear, tools and kitchen equipment. It was not hard. I also helped the electricians to repair heating elements for the camp's kitchen or for the garrison office. My boss, Ernst Bonke, was a middle-aged German shoemaker from Gildehaus, a small village in Lower Saxony. He worked in his own small shop with one helper. During the war, he had been drafted to serve as a shoe repairman for an SS unit.

I had to move from my old barrack and sleep in a smaller one reserved only for those working in the kitchen, the hospital or the maintenance unit or those driving trucks to pick up camp supplies. My new neighbour was a young German sergeant named Hans. He had driven a tank during the war and now drove one of the camp's trucks. We actually became good friends. From time to time, he gave me some extra food – an apple or a piece of salted, frozen fish – or some soap. Because he was on the road all day long, I collected his lunch, which meant extra food for me. Sometimes I gave this to my friend Jozsi, or others. Hans acquired various special items when he was working outside the camp, and hid his loot under his mattress. The guards conducted search raids a few times during the month, usually in the daytime, looking for knives, stolen articles and vodka. I slept during the day, along with the rest of the night-shift workers, but whenever I heard a search party coming, I moved over to Hans's mattress and pretended to sleep. They never searched his bed.

The night shift of our maintenance unit started work after supper. At midnight, three or four people from the unit went to the kitchen to pick up our lunch. It was better food and almost double the usual portion given during the daytime. One Sunday at noon, I went for my regular meal and then, after a short while, I went back with Hans's food container because he happened to be sleeping at this time of day. A German member of the kitchen staff approached me while I was waiting in line. He didn't ask any questions, just slapped me hard across my face and yelled, "You are a cheater, a s**t Jew!" and other insults. He snatched the food container and kicked it away with his heavy boots. It broke.

Returning to the barrack, I told Hans what had happened. He was furious. We went to the kitchen, and Hans grabbed the German, punched him to the ground, breaking his nose. Hans forced him to apologize to me. The German did so, apologized to Hans, too, ran to the supply room and came back with a brand new food container. From then on, I never had to wait in line to pick up my food, even when this man was not on duty. News travelled fast!

During the night shift, the only language spoken was German. I had learned a little in school in Kisvárda, but here I had a crash course. In the six months I was in the maintenance unit, I learned a fair bit of German, though not enough to become fluent.

In September 1946, I was transferred to the transportation unit connected to the construction company. Now, it was Ukrainian that I heard spoken around me all day long. One worker, a local man, taught me, and I learned fast. I had no other choice. It was easy to learn and I became trilingual, but reading proved difficult, as the Cyrillic alphabet is hard to learn.

The house-building group worked as on an assembly line. First the earth-digging unit made the foundation of a house, mostly by hand, along with the aid of a few small machines. Once they finished one foundation, they moved on to dig the next one. The order was to build a long street with small houses on both sides. After the foundation was laid, the concrete workers poured cement for the basement. Another unit erected the wood frames of the walls and installed the window and door frames. Bricklayers and roofers worked simultaneously with the plumbers and electrical crews.

About twenty-five people and I transported the materials needed for each phase. My section delivered the window and door frames. There was a problem in that the section producing the dried wood frames fell behind most of the time. I often took the frames half dry, and the workers installed them immediately in order to meet the quota. The window panes were installed, but when the new owners moved into their houses, many of them were unable to open the windows. Some windows that did open could not be closed. The homeowners had to do a lot of repair work, but nobody complained. The

Soviet communist government had given them a home, and they were content.

Everybody stole. At the end of the working day, both the members of my unit and the locals walked home with a piece of firewood, a few nails, a brick or a little white paint. The guards were watching us, but they did the same thing.

Throughout the cold, windy winter of 1946, the work continued, but at a much slower pace. One day, about three hundred people, including the thirty-two Jews, were ordered to report to a special barrack. More winter clothing and an extra ration of bread, sugar and *machorka* were handed out to each of us. Then, armed guards escorted us to the railroad station. Nobody knew where we were headed, not even the guards. To our surprise, in the cattle cars we boarded, there were drum heaters and plenty of bunks and toilet pails. With regular stops and food distribution, the trip took six days. Our destination turned out to be Kursk, a city in Russia where a large tank battle had taken place during the war.

When we arrived in Kursk, I heard it referred to as the "windy city." No wonder! As we left the train, we had to hold onto one another in order not to be blown away. The temperature was -30°C. As standard procedure, before entering our barracks, we had to go through the debugging and sanitation process again. We hung all our clothes up, after removing every comb, wooden utensil or piece of paper, so that the clothes could be sterilized by heat. Naked, we ran to another room, where it was warmer. We each received a tiny piece of soap, a small towel and a pot with about three litres of hot water. It wasn't much, but at least the water was not frozen. After about fifteen minutes, the heat-room door opened, and we hoped to get back into our now hot and clean clothing. But somebody had left flammable material in a pocket, the clothes had started to burn and then the whole heat-room caught fire. People opened the doors on both sides. The smoke was so thick that we couldn't see a thing. All the clothes were destroyed. We had to choose between dying from smoke inhalation inside or braving the severe cold outside. Someone broke the small window, and sixty to seventy naked men started to run to a nearby building, which was an unheated office. Luckily, the door was open, and the staff supplied us with blankets. We stuck together in threes and rolled the blankets around us.

About one hour later, we were issued replacement clothing in various shapes, colours, sizes and conditions. My pants were four sizes too large, the jacket two sizes too small and the overcoat a foot too long. The boots were so huge that I had to stuff two pairs of socks into each one to be able to walk. I looked elegant indeed. Clad in my new outfit, I was still shaking from the cold and extremely hungry. We were given hot soup – with one refill – a bowl of thick barley and a slice of black bread, which made me feel as if I were in heaven.

The new accommodation was an old, refurbished barrack. There were 200 to 250 of us packed into one room, which had two or three small windows on each wall, close to the ceiling. In the middle of this room was a big, red-brick oven. The only heating material was brown peat, which burns slowly with low heat. We took turns standing close to the oven; after warming our fronts and then our backs, we'd run to the bunks to try to retain the warmth under the blankets. The bunks were close to the walls, and the room temperature was only a bit above the freezing point. To stay warm, we slept in threes, close to one another in the spoon position, piling our three blankets on top of us to keep relatively warm. Turning over? No problem. All three of us would turn in unison to face the opposite direction.

One major problem was supplying water for the kitchen, and for drinking and washing. The only source of water was a well about 250 metres away, across a field. Ten people, hauling a large sled to which four barrels were tied, were assigned to go there. These people tied ropes around their waists and to one another because the cold temperatures, extremely strong wind and icy field made the task not only difficult but dangerous. One man fell, and the rope slipped away from his waist. He was blown away and nobody was able to help him. The soldiers found him days later, frozen to death.

The group carried axes to cut through the ice covering the well and filled the barrels with pails of water as fast as they could. They had to avoid splashing water on themselves, because it froze on their bodies within a few seconds. Making one round trip took more than an hour. I had to get water a few times and once, while filling the barrels, I fell down into an ice-covered puddle and my gloves became wet. By the time we arrived back at the kitchen, all my fingers were frozen. With the help of the cook and some warm water, we peeled off the gloves. Although the cook put warm oil on my fingers, I developed Raynaud's disease. Whenever the weather is cold, all my fingers turn snow white because of insufficient blood circulation, even if I am wearing warm, insulated gloves. When the blood circulation slowly returns to my hands, it is very painful. Cold water on my fingers has the same effect. I will never forget that winter as long as I live.

Counting the Days

Spring came early, bringing ankle-deep mud and making the trips to fetch water even longer. Since April was mostly sunny, we were at least able to sleep individually. And the work was light: helping in the kitchen, repairing buildings, cleaning roads, getting water and gathering firewood. Change was in the air, and there was some talk about moving to another camp. Nevertheless, the morning head count continued. It became such a ritual that when I later went home to Budapest, for the first few days I actually felt like something was missing.

Around the middle of May 1947, after the head count, an officer called the names of Captain David, Lieutenant Jani and about a dozen other people. It was the first time that they had been called by their rank. The officer broke the good news to them: an order from Moscow had come, and they were going home right away. What a cheer broke out! A truck was waiting for them, and after a lot of tearful hugging, kissing and well-wishing, they were on their way. We, the remaining Jews, felt a little empty. After being together with them for such a long time, we had become like brothers. David had been instrumental to our well-being and, in the final analysis, he would be to our freedom as well.

The camp officer who delivered the news to David and Jani told us that soon more names would be called. For the following three days, we slept little but dreamed a lot. Then the calls came: my name and more than fifty other Hungarians, including Jozsi Kohn and Leslie Frankel. Tears streamed down my face. I wondered if I would have a future after all or if I was only dreaming.

At the railroad station, I expected to see cattle cars. Instead, real passenger cars – albeit old and rusty – were waiting for us. Instead of pails, we had a private washroom. What luxury! We were to travel like human beings. The train took us to Kiev, the capital city of Ukraine on the banks of the Dnieper River. We were taken to a camp on the outskirts of the city. After a welcome shower and a fine shave, we ate a decent supper. The well-stocked camp supply room, full of men's clothing, gave us the chance to dress in civilian clothes in the appropriate sizes. We then enjoyed a good night's sleep in a clean room.

On June 1, after four days of rest and food, trucks transferred us to the railroad station. We did not have to go on foot! During our trip across the city, I noticed bombed-out buildings and missing power lines. Repair brigades were everywhere. New water and sewer lines were being laid down. Before we took our places in the old Pullman train, we were given full meals, each with one extra slice of bread. All the passengers on the train were Hungarians full of hope; the train would travel toward the West!

It was late evening when the steam engine started to pull the train. We slept anywhere we could: on the benches, the floor and even on the luggage nests. Every door was guarded, which, we were told, was for our own protection, to prevent an attack by locals who hated foreigners. There had been a few attacks before.

At the end of the train, there was a cattle car carrying our food supply. The train stopped periodically to take up water and coal, and at the same time, we received our daily three meals. I volunteered to distribute food and water to my unit. The distribution unit, including me, ate first. Then, when the train stopped, the rest of the people and the guards ate. During the war, the United States had sent supplies, including canned food, to help the starving Soviet population. The

Soviets took most of the supplies but didn't trust the canned food. For us, it was the best treat. We cut open the one-gallon cans containing cooked ham, corned beef or other meat. We also had dill pickles, bread, coffee and sugar. This tasted like a five-star gourmet meal.

Nine days after we left Kiev we arrived in Záhony, the town on the border with Hungary. We had to change trains there because Soviet gauge railroad tracks were a little wider than those in Europe. A new Hungarian flag was flying, and Hungarian-speaking border guards were waiting for us. During the changeover, I met a man from Kisvárda, and I asked him to contact my uncle Erno to tell him I was alive and had arrived in Hungary.

Our Red Army guards soon left, saying, "Do svidaniya." (See you again.) I said, "Never!" I had arrived at the camp in Ukraine on June 13, 1945. Almost two years later, I was released from the camp, and I arrived back in Hungary on June 13, 1947. It proved to be a lucky day, indeed. We arrived at the main railroad station of Debrecen two days later. Armed Hungarian soldiers took over the security and led us to the eating area of an empty army camp. It had been a long time since I had sat on a chair at a table and eaten with a fork and knife. An army doctor advised us not to jump on the food and overeat. Hungarian food contains a lot of fat, mostly lard, and he said our bodies had to adjust to the different food.

In the dressing room, we exchanged our clothing for even better civilian clothing from a large depot. My outfit consisted of a pair of clean grey pants, which had a small repair on one leg, and a nice jacket in my size, made from expensive material. On the left pocket, I noticed small holes that must have remained after the removal of the yellow Star of David. The jacket had been worn by a Jew!

We were permitted to go outside the camp but not into the city. I went with my friend Jozsi and three others to a nearby street for a walk, just to experience our long-awaited freedom. It was a strange feeling, walking without armed guards, a feeling beyond description. When we passed by a little house, an elderly woman invited us in for a snack. Her husband, she told us later, had not come home from the Eastern front, and she felt pity for young people returning from the war. She put a big pot of Hungarian stuffed cabbage with a thick layer of sour cream on the table. Neither Jozsi nor I took any of this heavy food. However, the three others each ate a fairly large portion. I asked for a glass of milk, a piece of white bread and a hard-boiled egg. After eating, we hugged the kind woman and offered our heartfelt thanks. The next day, all three of the men who had eaten the heavy meal became sick, and we took them to the city hospital. One of them died shortly after.

One day, somebody called my name after breakfast and led me to the office of a young lady. She told me to go with her to the city's teaching hospital. The research department at the hospital had been sent a medical report from the Soviet camp explaining my condition. The attending physician told me that I'd had a terrible case of furunculosis (boils) in addition to scurvy. After a thorough examination, the doctor took blood and urine samples. Then he injected me with an antibiotic.

When I returned to the camp, there were forty to fifty people waiting to leave. They were from Debrecen or nearby. Among them was my old buddy Leslie Frankel. He had lived in Debrecen before the war with his three sisters, and he gave me their addresses so that I could visit. After a bittersweet goodbye, we promised to keep in touch.

Another fifty to sixty names were called right after lunch, including mine. I was given a one-way train ticket to Budapest and a month's pass for that city's transportation system. Uniformed Hungarian officers and a man in civilian attire welcomed us back to the free and socialist Hungary. The man in civilian clothes, who I presumed was also an officer, delivered a speech that went something like this:

"You are free citizens. Your life was saved by the great Soviet Union. You were well treated in the Soviet camps. The best thing for your safety would be for you not to talk about life in the camps. If you are thinking of talking about any poor treatment or suffering in the

Soviet Union, think again! It would be anti-government propaganda. You don't want to become an enemy of the State! The new government knows how to deal with our enemies. Deportation and jail, with or without a trial, is the minimum anybody can expect. Enjoy your free state and work hard to make this socialist Hungary a strong country."

I took this warning seriously, and I didn't mention a word of my time in the Ukraine. I did not talk about it until I became a Canadian citizen. Some people didn't heed the warning and ended up in an internment camp in Kistarcsa.

After the speech, each of us was given a small duffle bag containing a set of spare underwear, a shaving kit with new razor blades, a half-loaf of bread and a piece of hard cheese. The camp office also supplied each of us with a new ID card. Trucks then took us to the railroad station. After saying goodbye to my friend Jozsi Kohn and others who were headed elsewhere, I boarded the train to Budapest. After three years of suffering, I was free of German soldiers, free of discrimination; I could walk freely as a Jew! Or so I believed.

The train was full of farmers who were going to Budapest to exchange produce for clothing or other items. Bartering prevailed over the use of the new Hungarian currency, the forint. One of the farmers glanced at my jacket with the little holes and obviously recognized that the yellow Star of David had been removed. I overheard him tell his friend, "I think more Jews came back than we sent to the Germans, and the Jews are talking about death camps and killing." His friend replied, "Not only that, but they have the guts to claim back their stores and even their houses."

I was shocked to hear these antisemitic remarks. I had come home to be free, to be welcomed and to live without fear. But times hadn't changed, and hatred still flourished. When I stood up, they were quiet. I said nothing, just looked into their eyes, ready to punch them. There was not a sound until we arrived at Nyugati, the western station of Budapest.

I rushed to Klauzál Square to our last home address to try to find my mother and sister. I believed that my father had died on the Eastern front in 1943 after the government had sent my mother notification to that effect. I arrived after 10:00 p.m., when the entrance of the apartment building was already locked, a common practice in Budapest. I rang the bell and the superintendent opened the door. I told him I had lived there before the war, and he let me in to talk to the people who were living in our old apartment. They told me that after liberation, the city's housing department had given the apartment to families who needed shelter. My mother and sister had returned home, but several weeks later were assigned to a shared apartment elsewhere. The new tenants didn't know their address.

At least I knew that my mother and sister were alive, but I still didn't have a home. It was late. The only other address that I knew was that of the Rosners, Ibolya's family, on Baross Street. The superintendent there knew me and let me in. My heart was galloping as I rang their bell. I wondered who would open the door and whom I would find alive. Kati, Ibolya's mother, opened the door. Right behind her was Klara, her sister, Tibor's mother. For a long time we just hugged one another, tears running freely down our faces. I was thinking about how to tell Kati of Andrew's death without breaking her heart. We sat down and millions of questions followed. Finally, I told them that Andrew had died of kidney failure at the camp. Kati started hitting me and yelling, "Why didn't you take care of him? It was your responsibility and you let him down!" Gradually she calmed down, and it was my turn to ask what had happened to Ibolya. She was unable to answer me. Klara told me the tragic story: Ibolya had been sent on a forced march, along with other Jewish women, from one of the death camps near the end of the war. She was very ill and was admitted to a hospital in March 1945. In April, an armed unit entered the hospital, which was full of Jewish women, and killed them one by one on their sick beds. Only one girl survived to tell the Red Army officials what had happened, once the district was liberated. Ibolya had been murdered at twenty-one years old. I was silent for a long time.

Then Klara and Kati told me about Tibor. After our escape from the camp in Budapest in October 1944, Tibor had headed home. But soon after, the Arrow Cross had raided his house and found him. He was taken to a westbound marching unit but was too weak to keep up with the group. When a Hungarian soldier saw him sitting on the side of the road, he shot him dead.

Klara and Kati told me that they had hidden on a farm during the last months of the war. Four months after finally returning home, John Rosner had died of a liver infection. It seemed there was no end to the devastating news. The Nemes family – Ibolya's uncle Ernő; his wife, Anna; and their twin girls – who had been living as gentiles, had nonetheless had to prove their origins when the Germans occupied Hungary in March 1944. Everybody had to do so, going back to their grandparents. Ernő subsequently lost his job, and his daughters were thrown out of their parochial school. When they learned that they were of Jewish origin, the girls even contemplated suicide. Ernő was sent to a forced labour camp, where he had to wear a white armband. Later, he was sent to the front. Nobody knew what happened to him. Close to Ernő and Anna's home, on Mátyásföld, there was a small air-field for local traffic, which was used by the military. The Allied forces destroyed the field and, with it, the Nemes family home. Anna and the girls died in the bomb shelter.

I later found out that my father's sisters Margit and Frida were alive, but Frida's husband, Miklós, who was my mother's younger brother, had been sent to a forced labour camp and then to the Eastern front, where he died. My father's brother Frank and his wife, Gizi, had survived. After the war, they made their way to a DP camp in Germany and eventually managed to immigrate to the United States, settling in Philadelphia. They had two daughters, Kathy and Rosalie; both later married, and each have two children.

I found out from Kati and Klara that after liberation my mother and sister had resided at Klauzál Square 6, the building next door to our old apartment. My sister, Barbara, had married Geza Fleischacker, who was involved in a lot of black-market business. Since the police were after him, my mother, Barbara and Geza left Hungary in a hurry in the fall of 1945 and headed to Germany to try to emigrate out of Europe. I also learned that my father was alive, in spite of the government's notification, but the Rosners didn't know his address and had seen him only once.

The night passed quickly, full of talk and heartbreaking news. These two women, who had both lost their husbands and their children, asked me to stay and live with them. I told them I had to find my own peace and needed time to heal my wounds. I promised to stay in close contact with them.

After a quiet breakfast, I went to Klauzál Square 6 and inquired after my mother. The superintendent directed me to apartment unit 9, where my mother, sister and brother-in-law had lived. A woman opened the door, and after I explained who I was, she invited me in. She didn't have much to tell me, but she was able to give me my mother's address in Germany. My mother had left a few things behind: an old pair of shoes, a woman's coat and a pair of men's pyjamas. I took only the pyjamas. These had been mine before the war and were my only remaining possession.

After leaving the apartment, I sat on a bench in the nearby park and watched people. They came from somewhere and they went somewhere. They came from somebody and went to somebody. Perhaps they were rushing home to their family. And me? Nowhere to go, nothing to do and nobody waiting for me. I was free and I was home, but I felt so alone. I wasn't feeling hopeful about starting a new life. What had I survived for?

Alone

I decided to return to the Rosners, the only place that offered a bed, warm food and people to talk to. On my walk there, I was surprised to see so many damaged buildings, some of them supported by wooden pillars. A few apartment buildings were half destroyed, but people still found nooks in them to live in. Budapest was in ruins. The bridges were down, the factories unusable and apartment and government buildings bombed out. There were shortages of food, clothing, housing and construction materials.

In the Rosners' house, we talked all that day and almost all night about things of the past and the future. The next day, I went to the office of the Hebrew Immigrant Aid Society (HIAS). There, I received some documents concerning my time spent in forced labour camps and an application form for a three-week stay in a sanatorium, a health spa. I found an old suitcase in their warehouse and, with their permission, filled it up with clothing that had been donated. I was also given a new shaving kit, towels and a bag of real coffee, sugar, soap, milk powder and sardines, all from the United States.

I then sat in the HIAS dining room with two other men who had also just returned home from a POW camp. The homemade meal, which included white bread, tasted delicious. During the meal, a tall, well-dressed man came to our table and introduced himself as Dr. Zoltan Klar, the editor of the *Társadalmunk* (*Our Society*) daily newspaper. He wrote down our names and asked a lot of questions about our situation. He asked us why we were there and whether we needed all those things the HIAS had given us. We told him the truth: yes. Our answers to questions about our health seemed to upset him. He gave us a small amount of money and left.

When I told the story to the Rosners, they informed me that Zoltan Klar and his newspaper opposed the government and took any opportunity to slam it. The following day, the *Társadalmunk* carried a front-page story with the headline "How The Present Coalition Government Neglects Its Citizens Who Need A Great Amount Of Help, Including Those Who Just Returned From The POW Camps." The story included our names, along with the comment, "Those poor, suffering people have to beg for clothing and food. They need immediate medical help, but the government does nothing about it," After seeing our names in the paper, I regretted speaking to Zoltan Klar.

However, when I went to the office of the Ministry of Health with my application, I was treated royally. They had read the newspaper, too! In short order, my application was accepted. I was given a voucher to the sanatorium of Hajdúszoboszló, famous for its hot spa and healing treatments, for a three-week stay with accommodation, food and all treatments paid for by the government. I also received a return train ticket, two theatre tickets and six entrance passes to a nearby entertainment centre. I was given a wallet containing about 100 forint in spending money. The starting date for my stay at the sanatorium was ten days away.

I practically flew back to tell the Rosners about it. I couldn't believe my good fortune. We were sitting down to supper when the bell rang. Kati went to open the door, and I heard a man greet her with, "Hello! I am Sándor Vajda. Do you remember me? I am Leslie's father!" When he entered the room, I almost fainted. My father casually greeted Klara and me. I stood up, wanting to embrace him as a son who hadn't seen his father for five years. Before I could open my mouth, he confronted me, asking, "Why didn't you come to my house? I am your father! Your uncle Erno called me and told me you had come back from the Soviet Union."

When I had a chance to speak, I told him we had received notification of his death from the Hungarian government in 1943. Then he told us his story: In 1943, after the Eastern front had been broken through, he had joined the Soviet partisans, along with several others, and helped by keeping their camp in order, cooking for them and cleaning. Then they were sent to Siberia to work in a factory. He had returned to Hungary at the end of 1945 and found only the postcard that I had written to my mother while in quarantine at the camp. He learned that my mother and sister had left Hungary for Germany. As was common among Jewish survivors after the war, he decided to change his surname, which became Vajda. He had also remarried.

My father ordered me to pack and go with him. I knew how to follow orders from a stranger, but orders coming from my father now were hard to take. I could do without his affection, but his cold, cruel attitude made me fall silent. We left and started walking to his apartment.

In Hungary at the time, there was a strictly enforced law that residents had to register their permanent or temporary address at the nearest police station. The superintendent of an apartment building signed the registration for its tenants; hotels registered their guests. Moving to a new address necessitated deregistering from the old address and registering for the new one. I had not registered when I went to the Rosners' apartment, not knowing if I would stay. On our way to my father's house, he took away my ID card to take care of the registration. That way, I wouldn't have to explain at the police station why I hadn't registered before.

My father's home was on Dohány Street, in a half-destroyed apartment building. The large three-bedroom apartment was divided into two separate units. Another couple occupied one bedroom and a small "nanny's room." We all shared the same entrance and bathroom. My father introduced me to his wife, Margit Ungar, who greeted me with a friendly welcome. Before the war, the whole apartment had been her family's residence.

I spent the first night in the dining room, on the extra bed, wondering how this arrangement would work out. The next day during breakfast, my father and Margit asked me a lot of questions, and I, in turn, asked them a few. My father told me that when he returned to Budapest, he had found both our home and our factory destroyed. He went to live in the apartment where my mother and sister had lived before leaving the country, found out their address in Germany and started to exchange letters with my mother, each one nastier than the last. He asked them, and then ordered them, to return to Hungary. My mother wanted him to join her. Both my parents blamed each other for the previous difficult, stormy nineteen years of marriage. Each refused to join the other. He filed for divorce. Since he had friends with connections, the court quickly granted it.

My father became friendly with Imre Ungar, a charming man, who introduced him to his parents and three of his sisters. One of them was Margit, a Jewish widow who had lost her husband in the war. She didn't have any children. My father and Margit married a few weeks later.

In one of the letters to my mother, my father asked her (and later asked me) what had happened to our upholstered living-room chairs. He hadn't told anyone, not even his wife, that he had hidden jewellery and money under the slipcovers. My mother kept on saying that she didn't know anything about the chairs. Our apartment was inside the ghetto in 1944, and the poor occupants had likely burned everything to heat the place. My father didn't believe my mother and accused her of stealing his jewellery. I knew nothing about his treasure, but he refused to believe me, too.

The next few days were difficult. The only thing that relieved the tension was a family supper at which I was introduced to the Ungar family. I met Margit's father, mother, brothers and sister, Aranka. Although my father, mother, sister and I had all survived the Holocaust, we did not have a family; I was without a real home.

It was soon time for me to go to the sanatorium of Hajdúszoboszló. Nobody asked me to come back, and I was relieved to be out of the house. The train was almost full, but with my one suitcase, I found a window seat. I looked out at the fields passing by, farmers tending to their crops, owners painting their houses and children going to school. It painted a peaceful picture, which I was not part of. After a while, some passengers opened their baskets and bottles and, following the Hungarian tradition, started eating and drinking. Jokes were flying. I had nothing – no food, no drink and no jokes. But they invited me to join the party, so I arrived at Hajdúszoboszló in a good mood.

On the first day, I was given a complete checkup, including an examination, X-rays, and blood and urine tests. A skin specialist and a physiotherapist looked after me. The food and the service were first class. There was a full breakfast early each day. One hour later, the treatments started. The whole package included physiotherapy, ultrasound and shortwave therapy, mud-pack sessions and massage, though not all on the same day. The treatment followed a strict medical regimen, and I ended most days in the thermal pool. The medical director had received a report from the hospital in Debrecen with the results of my tests. I was given injections and pills – perhaps they were vitamins – to eliminate all the blisters and prevent new boils from forming. I had to eat a lot of fruits and vegetables. I felt I was under the best of care.

During my stay at the sanatorium, I occasionally went to a restaurant in the city, a place with live music and dancing under the summer sky. I had been a good dancer before the war, and I loved dancing. On several evenings, I noticed a beautiful young woman in a wheelchair, being pushed by her parents. When they arrived at their table, she stood up, took a few steps and then sat on a regular chair all evening. I saw her feet tapping to the rhythm of the music. I learned that they lived in Hajdúszoboszló, and many people knew and greeted them.

On the last evening of my stay, I went to their table and introduced myself. As was customary in Europe, I asked the parents to allow me to dance with their daughter. For a few seconds there was silence. Then the mother whispered to the young woman, "Go," and said to me, "Yes! With pleasure!" The young woman stood up, holding my hand, and we slowly walked to the dance floor. The band was playing a lovely tango, my favourite dance. She was a little shaky when I put my arm around her. We started dancing. One minute later, we were the only couple on the floor. Everybody was sitting down, watching us. I saw her parents and others with tears streaming down their faces.

She told me she had been studying to become a ballet dancer, but when she was twelve, polio struck. Almost five years passed, full of painful treatments. Nobody, including her doctor, had any hope that she would be able to walk again. She listened to music all the time. She said that she would be turning seventeen next week and this dance was her best birthday gift ever and she hoped it would be the turning point in her recovery. I felt honoured to dance with her and to be able to make her smile.

When the music stopped, we walked back to the table and I expressed my heartfelt thanks. Her mother hugged me and repeatedly thanked me, with tears in her eyes. On the way back to my room, I realized I had forgotten to ask the young woman's name. I don't know what happened to her. Did she recover fully? Become a dancer, a wife and a mother? I hope she did it all.

$\sim$

At the end of my treatment, I made a decision to join my uncle Erno in Kisvárda. I called him, and he was excited about my visit. Erno and his wife, Anna, were waiting for me at the railroad station in Kisvárda. The streets, the houses and the stores gave me an uneasy feeling. During my stay in Kisvárda, I never went to see any of the houses my family had lived in, not even my grandmother's place. The *gimnázium* was the only building I went to see. During the war, it had been bombed and suffered extensive damage.

Uncle Erno, who had changed his last name to Vamos, had rented a small apartment in a house that had a large vegetable garden. He married Anna only after the war but they had been engaged for eight years prior to that. He and Anna didn't have children. I slept on the extra bed in their bedroom. Erno took care of reporting my change of address to the authorities. My mother wrote to me almost every week and sometimes my sister wrote too, urging me to leave the country. They were waiting for visas to go to the United States. My mother's brother Alex had sent her an affidavit of sponsorship from Brooklyn.

Erno had his own shop across the street from his house, where he made customized uppers for shoemakers. Back then, the footwear selection in stores was limited, especially in small cities. Anybody who had a wider or narrower foot than the average, or was between the standard sizes, had to order made-to-measure shoes or boots. Erno's business was successful, employing five or six people, and I started to work in his shop. I had a place to sleep, food to eat and clean garments; I had almost everything.

Uncle Erno never wanted to speak to me about what had happened to him and Anna during the war. I knew only that he had been in the army and in and out of forced labour camps. He often said to me, "I want to forget every place, all the people. I don't want to be buried under all the ashes of my memories. I want to look forward, not back." But I wanted to know what had happened to my grandmother, and I kept asking him. Eventually, he told me that she and some others in Kisvárda had been marched to the outskirts of the city by the Hungarian gendarmerie. They were locked into an old, empty wooden barn, and then the barn was set on fire. No one survived. My uncle heard this from someone who witnessed it. The rest of the Jews in Kisvárda were deported to Auschwitz.

The Jewish population of Kisvárda had numbered 3,770 in 1941. In 1946, there were only 804 Jews remaining. The survivors soon moved away to larger cities or other countries. By 1953, there were 355 Jews and by 1999, hardly any Jews lived in the city.

Erno began to search for somebody who could secretly assist me to get out of Hungary to Austria. Right after the war, it had been easy to leave the country, but as the new communist government established itself, the border patrols became better organized. You could end up in jail for either trying to leave or helping somebody to do so. Just inquiring about leaving could result in a visit by the Államvédelmi Osztály (ávo), the State Security Department. And it cost a lot of money to pay smugglers, money I didn't have.

One day I was working in the vegetable garden, removing large stones, debris and tall weeds. As I dug out a stone from under a tree, I found a small cigar box. Inside, I discovered quite a treasure: three gold rings, each with a small diamond; eight or nine gold necklaces; three gold cameo medallions; and a gold pocket watch. Erno told me that the Jewish family who had owned and lived in the house hadn't come back after the war; the whole family had perished in a concentration camp.

This is how I got money to pay my way out of Hungary. Erno kept the watch and Anna one necklace. We sold the rest on the black market. We ordered a pair of made-to-measure shoes for me, and Erno made a cavity in the heels of the shoes to hide money. In each heel we put a US five-dollar bill that I would use to buy Austrian schillings.

In the middle of December 1947, Erno found a man who would pick me and another man up in Budapest and escort us to the border. A woman would hold all the money due to him until I sent back the password indicating that I was in Austria. I filled a backpack with a minimal amount of clothing and went to see the Rosners in Budapest. They were glad to see me but sad to learn that the purpose of my visit was to say goodbye.

The time was set for my escort to come to their apartment on December 26, 1947. At noon, I was ready to go. A few minutes past noon, I looked down from the third-floor window to see if my escort was coming, and I saw him with another man in front of the entrance. I was about to run down to join them. Just then, a black, unmarked car stopped, and three individuals in civilian clothes stepped out, put handcuffs on both men and pushed them into the car. The car sped away. The whole thing took less than two minutes.

It took a few minutes for me to recover. I sat down to discuss the situation with the Rosners. I could not go back to Kisvárda, since the authorities might be looking for me there or even here in Budapest. I decided to stay indoors for a few days.

When I called Erno to wish him happy New Year, he already knew that the men had been taken to the ÁVO headquarters. The woman holding the payment money had also been arrested. I later found out that the escort man was sentenced to ten years in prison, the woman twelve years. The other man was in jail for five years.

Once again, I had no place to go. I had to report my new address, but I didn't know where it would be. I was safe for a few days because so many people travelled around the New Year. The address report could wait until after New Year's Day. I called my father's number and talked to his wife, Margit. She invited me to move to their apartment until I found a place to rent. I accepted the invitation; at least I would be safe concerning the change-of-address report.

Four days after New Year's, I moved back to my father's house. Erno sent the belongings I had left behind. He wasn't thrilled with my decision, but I told him it would be a temporary solution. My father didn't seem too happy to see me, but he didn't say a word. I tried to avoid arguments on any subject. We didn't talk much, and certainly not about my mother or Erno.

The day after moving back to my father's place, I went to the leather industry union to ask for work. The next day, I started working in a small, privately owned shoe factory as a leather cutter. There were three other cutters, and we were all paid by the piece. To earn extra money, we took home work to do on Saturdays and Sundays. Monday morning, we returned the cut pieces to the factory. One Friday around noon, when we were getting ready to go home, two detectives showed up at the door. They told the cutters, including me, to stay. When all the other workers had left, the detectives ordered us to take off our jackets and shirts. I was surprised to see that each of the three other cutters had one or two large pieces of material tied to his chest. We all had to go to the police station. The detectives filled out a police report on the three men. Four detectives went to search their apartments for stolen material and found some in their homes. I hadn't saved any material, and therefore had nothing in my home. I was released while the others had to stay at the police station overnight. They were charged for stealing material and selling it on the black market.

After the detective had left my father's apartment, my father was upset, even though the detective had found nothing and had apologized to him. When I returned home, my father almost killed me for being the reason a detective had come to his house and for putting him in a suspicious light. I told him the story and explained how innocent I was, but he wouldn't listen. Margit came home, and they argued about my continuing to stay with them. My father told me that I had to move out the following week. Aranka, Margit's sister, came to my rescue and offered me a room in her apartment, which was in the same building. I moved out in five minutes flat.

I continued working at the shoe factory. In March 1948, I went to a leather workers' union party at the head office. One of the section directors of the union, Geza Kocsis, called me over. He seemed glad to see me, asked what I was doing and told me to come by his office the next day. It hit me that I knew Geza from somewhere, and then I remembered that we had attended the same trade school. He had been a slow learner and I had helped him, mostly with mathematics and pattern making. I had also often shared my lunch with him. He came from a Roma family and most of the other students kept their distance from him, so he obviously remembered me.

When I visited Geza in his office the next day, he explained a confidential program to me. In Hungary, there were fewer than a dozen large footwear factories and more than two dozen medium and small ones. The same situation existed for the leather tanneries. The communist government had nationalized all the factories, and in some medium or small factories, the government hired the former owners as production managers under the watchful eyes of a newly appointed government director.

In each factory, workers were union members and some were members of the Communist Party. There was a party secretary and a union secretary. Each factory had its own production, shipping, payroll and accounting system. The cost of production varied so much that in some places the same footwear might cost 50 per cent more or 50 per cent less. The Ministry of Labour wanted to re-organize every factory so that there would be a standard system for the whole country. They knew there would be a slight difference in each region because of the training and experience of the local labour force, as well as the living standard of each region, both of which affected the labour cost.

To accomplish its goal, the ministry needed trained and trustworthy industrial engineers with a great deal of knowledge in the leather and footwear industry. The government made an agreement with the University of Budapest to organize a six-month crash course for twenty-five to thirty candidates to be trained as industrial technicians. The government would provide all the tuition fees, school supplies, transportation costs and suppers. After five months, based on the results of the final exams, the government would select twelve students from the course to become industrial technicians. The students would receive a month's paid leave to study in the daytime for the final month of the course, on condition that they agree to work outside Budapest in any part of the country.

Geza offered me a place in the program and all the help I might need. I eagerly accepted his offer, ready to start a new life. My first session started in April 1948. The teaching staff outlined the course: Monday to Friday, the program would start at 6:30 p.m. and finish at 10:30 p.m. There would be three groups, rotating to different teachers and subjects. The training on Saturday and Sunday would be from 9:00 a.m. to 2:00 p.m. with further tutoring in the library until 4:00 p.m. We would study basic statistics and bookkeeping, work and time schedules, production organizing methods, mathematics and some algebra. A psychologist gave us a lecture once a week.

It was hard to study after a full day at work. Even so, I found every subject interesting, and I threw all my energy into learning. I didn't care about missing a social life. After five months of study, I was one of the twelve students chosen to continue the final month of education. On December 2, 1948, I graduated with high honours. Geza was very proud of me.

Around this time, my mother realized that I could not get to Germany and that I had to secure my future. The US Consulate had told my mother that she and my sister might have to wait five years for a visa. Since Israel had just recently become a country, they went there, along with other refugees. My mother, afraid I would neglect her and become my "father's boy," asked me not to take his name, Vajda, and I complied. I later applied for the new surname Vertes, which became official in 1950.

I started to work in the coal-mining city of Tata, west of Budapest, on December 8, 1948. I think I was the only Jew in the city. The majority of the local residents worked in the mining, service or transportation industries. The shoe factory, with about 350 workers, was on the outskirts of the city. The government had nationalized this factory, too, and hired the former owner as a cutting department foreman. He had a lot of knowledge in pattern making, cost calculation and leather cutting.

The whole factory was under the direction of Andrew Kovacs, who was appointed by the Ministry of Labour. Before the war, he had been a shoe factory worker. I was the new kid on the block; everybody greeted me politely, but with some reservation. They took me on a half-day orientation tour, introducing all the section foremen and forewomen, the local secretary of the Communist Party and the secretary of the union.

The next day, I asked for a meeting with the board of directors, the secretaries and all forepeople. I informed them about the purpose of my work, namely, to find ways to improve working conditions in order to eliminate material losses and increase labour efficiency. I tried to create a good impression and ease their worry that the out-of-town stranger would be detrimental to them. I assured them all that my work would be to their benefit.

My first step was to study the movement of materials in every department, and shipping methods. In the cutting room, using the national standards, I prepared a new detailed floor plan and an economical material flow chart. Cutting methods, tools, sizing, size markings and wages were compared to the national standards and adjusted. I then did the same in the other departments. My plan included exchanging unused machinery for needed machines.

After a month, my system was working smoothly, and I started to receive suggestions from the workers. During the next three months of hard work, sometimes including late evenings and weekends, I made a detailed study and came up with suggestions for the entire factory. I presented these to the ministry. Except for a few minor changes, they were satisfied with my report. The hardest part was explaining the whole plan to the directors and the workers.

The next project entailed developing a new payroll system and implementing the changes in the production lines. I loved my work. It gave me a chance to observe people and organize new operations. In the process, I also learned and tried to implement new and better methods. At the same time, I was teaching local people how to do my work so that they would be able to take over when I left for other assignments. When I left, the factory was in good hands.

I was then sent to a shoe factory in Szombathely, just over two hundred kilometres from Budapest, to organize one of its departments. One day, a message was waiting for me from Margit. She wrote that my father had had a gallbladder operation three days prior, and she thought I might like to know about it. Since leaving for Tata, I hadn't been to their home or spoken with my father. I was surprised that Margit had been able to track down my address.

A fellow worker was going to Budapest the next day with the factory truck, so I accompanied him and went to the hospital. On the way, I bought a leather wallet and a gold-tipped fountain pen for my father. Although a gallbladder operation was major surgery at that time, my father appeared to be in good shape. He greeted me sarcastically with, "How is Mr. Vertes?" He was obviously still miffed that I hadn't changed my name to Vajda. I greeted him with a quiet "Hello" and gave him my present. I asked him, "How is Mr. Vajda?"

"Fantastic," he replied. He talked about Margit, her family and his two new tailored suits. He told me that he and Margit would soon be going to a luxury hotel on Lake Balaton for two weeks of vacation. I was about to tell him about my work when an orderly came in to check the drainage bag. My father gave the wallet and fountain pen, which I had just given him, to the orderly as a gift. The orderly heartily thanked my father and left the room. After a few minutes of complete silence, I felt we had nothing else to talk about and that it was time for me to leave.

I had travelled hours for a twenty-minute visit. Some things never change.

~

I had only a few days' rest before starting my next project, in Debrecen. In June 1949, I implemented the same system in Debrecen as I had in Tata. This task was much easier because I had more experience and the factory had been well organized before the government national-ized it. I worked long hours and tried to help the people in the factory while being as pleasant as possible.

In early 1950, during an appointment with Geza Kocsis at the union office, I reported my progress at the various factories. Geza then asked me if I wanted to work in Budapest, and I accepted his of-fer. He gave me a name and an address where I could find a room to rent. That was to be the last time I saw Geza, my friend, helper and mentor. I organized all my files in Debrecen and turned over all the details to a young woman I had trained to take over my position. My transfer came in ten days. Shortly afterwards, a truck hit Geza's small car, killing him instantly. It was a terrible loss, and I felt awful for his family. He was so young.

∽

My next assignment was on the outskirts of Budapest, so I went to the address, in the city, that Geza had given me during our last meet-ing: 22 Rökk Szilárd Street. An elderly woman told me the room was already taken, but a family by the name of Ungar lived next door, and they had an extra room. I rang the bell, introduced myself and told them who had sent me.

Before the war, they had had a large three-bedroom apartment with a dining room. After the war, the city housing department had divided the apartment into two units, with separate entrances. The tenants shared both the toilet and the bathroom. Samuel and Serena Ungar had a small room, which they had converted into a kitchen, and a large bedroom. A door from there led to a furnished dining room that included a sofa. The rent was fair, so I rented this dining room. The next day I moved into their home, feeling alone again.

My assignment was in a large footwear factory called LeatherTex. It produced all kinds of footwear – from babies' shoes to the largest size of men's footwear. One of my friends had worked in this factory before, doing the same work as I did in Tata and Debrecen. He had to find other work because of eye-related problems. Since he had done a good job, it was easy to continue his work. I also found a few old friends in the factory's management with whom I worked well.

On my first Saturday with them, the Ungars invited me for dinner. We were eating and talking when, to my surprise, my father arrived. It turned out that Samuel was Margit's uncle, her father's brother. During their usual Friday evening meal, Samuel and Serena had told Margit and my father that they had a new tenant whose name was Leslie Vertes and that he worked in the footwear industry. My father and Margit knew immediately that their new tenant was me.

My father complained, loudly, that I hadn't gone to his place to live and that he'd had to find out from his in-laws that I was renting a place from the Ungars. I knew why he was talking like this: he wanted to show the Ungars that he was a caring father. We calmed him down, and a few minutes later we continued our dinner.

My Luck, My Destiny

I felt less pressure working at the LeatherTex footwear factory in Budapest. All my studies and experience were paying off, and for the first time in my life, I had an easy job. I was free every evening, so I joined an amateur theatre group. We performed some short plays and recited poems in different factories on their designated social evenings.

That summer, the factory's management was invited to the Scientific Society of Leather, Shoe and Allied Industries to participate in a three-day seminar to discuss ways to achieve better productivity. This society and more than a dozen others comprised the Federation of Technical and Scientific Societies, or, in Hungarian, Műszaki és Természettudományi Egyesületek Szövetsége (MTESZ) Since the subject of the seminar was my specialty, I participated in several sessions. On the closing evening, I praised the seminar's organizers for recognizing the importance of this subject matter. At the same time, I criticized them for their poor organization of the seminar itself.

A week later, I received an invitation to meet with Dr. Endre Valkó, the General Secretary of MTESZ. He said that three high-ranking officials had noticed my participation at the seminar. They already knew about my background and liked the work I had done in the last year and a half. MTESZ was in the process of establishing a new society for the sole purpose of gathering the best people in the country to make suggestions for improving productivity through better organization. Dr. Valkó offered me a full-time office job with a fair salary, which I accepted. My title was Secretary of the Society of Industrial Engineers and Organizers. I had been in the right place at the right time. I had two full-time and one part-time office staff. My direct boss was the vice-president of one of the largest industrial complexes, who worked as a volunteer in our organization. My job started around 10:00 a.m. and lasted sometimes until 11:00 p.m. Some days we had four or more workshops going on concurrently, which involved the participation of engineers, chartered accountants, financial officers and highly qualified production managers.

After my first year, MTESZ organized a five-day international convention. More than one thousand people came from countries around the world. My job entailed organizing buses to transport the participants from the hotels to the convention centres for workshops, to different restaurants and then back to their assigned hotels. I also organized tours for about three hundred spouses to museums in the city and to the countryside. This was the busiest and most rewarding job I ever had. I loved what I was doing, although it left no time for any social life.

In the summer of 1951, one of my co-workers, Judith Friedman, asked me if I was interested in changing my busy lifestyle a little to meet her long-time friend, Vera Neiser. I politely declined, saying I didn't have time for this. After her third try, I agreed to a double date with Vera, Judith and her boyfriend. Judith and I had spoken on June 13, my lucky day, and we arranged to go on a river supper-dance cruise three days later, on Saturday. During the cruise, I enjoyed having interesting discussions with Vera, and dancing with her.

The next few days, I kept thinking of Vera. A few days later, Judith asked, "So, Leslie, how did you like Vera?" I said she was lovely and I had enjoyed the evening with her. "Did you call her for a follow-up date?" she asked. When I said no, Judith gave me a lecture, and we planned another outing for the coming weekend. From then on, I had dates with Vera every weekend. As our friendship developed,

I learned about her life since childhood. She had grown up in Dombóvár with two younger sisters in a close-knit, loving family. Her father was hard working, well educated and intelligent. In 1940, when Vera was only eleven years old, breast cancer tragically claimed the life of her mother.

Around this time, Vera's father, Jozsef, like many others, wound up in a forced labour camp, leaving his three daughters in their grandmother's care. When he returned three months later, Jozsef realized that it was an impossible task for his mother to take care of the children. Eight months later, he married a woman named Elisabeth.

When Germany invaded Hungary, Vera and her family were deported to Auschwitz. Her grandmother was sent to the gas chambers. Vera was separated from her sisters and never saw them again. They, too, became victims of the Holocaust. Vera was sent to a labour camp in Germany with her stepmother, Elisabeth. The inhumane living conditions of the camp were indescribable. Vera's job making bombs in a munitions factory involved mixing and pouring hot sulphur into bombshells. This was hard work for an adult, but for a fifteen-year-old skinny, poorly fed girl, it was hell. Winter without proper shoes or a coat took its toll on her health.

When Vera and her stepmother were liberated in Germany in May 1945, they went back to Dombóvár, hoping to find some surviving relatives. Vera found only her father. Sixty-five of her family members had perished in different death camps. Jozsef had escaped from the labour camp and gone into hiding in Budapest. Vera's aunt Aranka and her husband, Rudi, who was a gentile, saved his life.

After the war, Vera needed a lot of medical attention. She found it very difficult to adjust to living without her sisters and grandparents. In 1948, her half-brother, Gabe, was born. He brought much joy to the family. Vera began working in a dressmaker's shop, but in a small town in Hungary, a young Jewish girl didn't have much of a future. She moved to Budapest to stay with her aunt Aranka, learned shorthand and other skills, and got an office job.

We spent more and more time together, and our friendship slowly developed into something greater. I had a hard time balancing my busy work schedule with my ever-increasing feelings toward her. In early August, I told Vera how I felt about her and asked her to marry me. Her answer was yes! We went to her aunt Aranka's place to celebrate our engagement on August 20, 1951.

We got married at City Hall in Budapest on January 12, 1952. My father, Margit, Vera's father and stepmother, Vera's aunt Aranka and her husband, Rudi, and Vera's uncle Ernest and his wife, Lulu, were witnesses to this event. After the wedding dinner, we went on a three-day honeymoon to a small bed-and-breakfast in Széchenyihegy, a beautiful hilly area in the twelfth district of Budapest.

After our short vacation, Vera moved into my room. The Ungars weren't crazy about the idea of having two people in the next room, but they wanted to help us. Using my office connections, I got the gas company to install an extra double burner in the Ungars' small kitchen, but it was still difficult for us to cook supper at the same time as Mrs. Ungar. There was no refrigerator, and we had to eat in our room. The Ungars even asked us to go to the bathroom together in order to disturb them less during the night.

There was a terrible shortage of housing in Budapest. I applied to so many places, but found nothing. We made applications in every district of the city for an apartment, but for some reason or another, we were rejected at every hearing. The situation seemed hopeless.

That same year, in June, I was drafted into the army for a three-month stint of military training. I had never liked the army, but I had to go, even though I reported that I was a newly married man. The camp was in the western part of the country. I have never been a physically strong person, and I found the training hard. During the army training, we had to learn how to throw a hand grenade. According to protocol, you pull the safety pin with your left hand, count to three and throw the grenade with your right hand. I was born left-handed, but my father had forced me to use my right hand because at that time, a left-handed person was unusual. I could use my right hand for most things, but I used my left hand to throw a ball. I explained to the drill sergeant that I could throw the grenade only with my left hand, but he insisted that I throw with my right.

Between the line of soldiers and the target board, there was a deep ditch for the sergeant to watch the grenade hit. I did as he told me: I pulled the pin with my left hand and threw the grenade with my right, but it went only halfway, landing right in front of the sergeant's ditch. He ducked, and when the grenade exploded just in front of the ditch, I knew I was in deep trouble. He accused me in court of nearly killing him. I told the judge my side of the story. I spent only three days in jail.

~

In July 1954, Vera became pregnant, which increased our urgency to find a home. We were still far down on the waiting lists, but we were desperate beyond description. The Ungars told us that we couldn't stay in their apartment any longer, and nobody was able to help us.

I told my work contacts about my fruitless apartment hunting. No one could promise anything, but they said they would try. Shortly after, Dr. Valkó, the General Secretary, called me to his office and informed me that the Hungarian Academy of Sciences had given us an apartment that belonged to them! He gave me two sets of keys and wished me all the best. This small but lovely apartment would not be ours to keep, but we could live there as long as I worked for my present organization.

I called Vera right away, and we rushed to the address: 6 Karthauzi Street. It was almost at the top of Svábhegy, Swabian Mountain, and we had to take a train up the mountain from the streetcar stop. We opened the door to our new apartment and were thrilled. Using a candle to light our way, we saw a small entry hall, a nice, full-sized bathroom, a large room and a balcony facing the mountain. There was no kitchen. There was central heat (very little) and central hot water (once a week for one hour). We said goodbye to the Ungars and moved our furniture and belongings to our new apartment. We made our small home very lovely. Using my connections, we obtained a double electric burner, and the entry hall became our kitchen.

We continually struggled to make ends meet. Even with both our salaries, we were always short of money by the end of the month. Vera had family from both her mother's and father's side who had immigrated to the US before the war and helped us enormously by sending us parcels with canned food and children's clothing. We had received a few sets of bed linen when we married. We sold things we could spare, like silk stockings.

When Vera's labour started, we went to Szent János Hospital in Buda. It was morning, and I left Vera in the hospital, believing her labour would last a while, perhaps until the evening. When I received a call after lunch that the baby was on the way, I rushed to the hospital, but they wouldn't let me into the delivery room. I had to wait in the lobby. When I called my office at about 5:00 p.m., they were surprised I didn't know the news: after a long labour, Vera had delivered a 9-pound baby boy. The nurses had forgotten to tell me, so I was the last person to know that I had become a father! That April 13, 1955, our lives changed forever.

A week later, I took Vera and our new son, George, home. Going into our apartment, I said to George, "You are a lucky one! You were born to hard-working parents. We welcome you with our hearts full of love!" George was a beautiful baby. My father and Margit came the next day with a crib, blankets, a small washtub and other useful items. My father grew to be a supportive, caring grandfather. Margit was also good to us. They visited us often, each time bringing some practical things for George. Vera's aunt Aranka and her husband, Rudi, also gave us a great deal of help and support.

Vera stayed home for six months to take care of our baby. Back then, there weren't any disposable diapers; we had to wash and iron all the cloth diapers. It took me an hour to get to work and even longer to get home. I tried to change my working hours, but it was difficult, and I had to do some work on most weekends.

After six months, Vera went back to work to keep her job with all its benefits, so we had to hire a woman to take care of George. Vera left for work early each morning. I waited at the door of our apartment at 9:00 a.m. for the caregiver to arrive, and then I rushed off to work. We had a busy, tiring life. George was our social life and our entertainment.

~

In October 1956, university students protested against the lack of freedom of speech in Hungary. They demanded that the Communist Party loosen up its strict censorship and let opposition voices be heard and the press report freely. The streets were full of yelling, marching protesters. Then the real riots started, against the police and, especially, the ÁVO, and high-ranking party officials. Street fights with guns and bullets made the daily news.

At Prime Minister Imre Nagy's request, the Red Army left Hungary, only to return in greater force a short time later. By early November, there was no chance that the uprising would succeed. The protesters' small firearms were no match for Soviet tanks. People were killed or wounded, and buildings were destroyed. Imre Nagy was arrested for treason and executed two years later. Looting and revenge ruled the day. The Jews were blamed for the atrocities committed by the communists in Hungary. True to Hungarian tradition, graffiti and signs were painted on walls. Some said, "We won't take you to Auschwitz " – meaning they would get rid of the Jews in their own country.

It was difficult to find food; transportation came almost to a standstill; and few people went to work. The border to Austria was open, and people fled by the thousands. After a long discussion, Vera and I decided that we should leave the country, too. Vera had close relatives in the United States: on her mother's side, there were her aunt Katy Roger and Katy's daughter, Suzy Rubin, and her family. On her father's side, there were Vera's aunts Rose Stone and Aranka Weltner and her husband. My mother's brother Alex, and my father's sisters Paula and Lena also lived in the States. My mother's brother Victor had died of polio in 1954, and my father's brother Albert had also passed away.

We thought it would be easy to obtain immigrants' visas to the United States, but first we had to flee Hungary. After careful investigation, I found a way to leave the country. I shared my escape plan with my friend Andrew Mahrer and his wife, who were the first to put the plan into action. With a forged travel document and pretending to be on official business, they travelled to Sopron, a city just inside the restricted border zone. From there, at night, which was the safest time, a farmer's son took them over the mountains to Austria. I received confirmation from them that they had arrived in Austria. We never saw them again, but we heard they went to England.

Then it was our turn to leave. We didn't say a word to anybody, not even to my father or Vera's father. We had George inoculated against smallpox by his doctor. We packed a few necessary things, mostly for George – clothing, diapers, food and some medication. On December 1, 1956, we left Budapest by train, with the border police checking our documents. We arrived in Sopron and slept in a cold local office for one night. When our escort arrived the next day, we started our ascent of the mountains. Despite the heavy rain and our fatigue, we forged ahead toward the border.

We were excited to see the Austrian flag about half a kilometre away, but then we heard loud talking and laughing. About twenty young Hungarians had just returned from Austria, and at that moment, the Hungarian border guards emerged from their hideouts and captured everybody. We pleaded with an older soldier to let us go, but he was afraid of his comrades. They put all of us on a train and took us to a building in the border city of Győr. Although the sign on the outside of the building read Red Cross, armed soldiers were stationed inside because it was, in fact, a jail. I put our travel documents in the pocket of George's winter coat. They searched us, interrogated me and confiscated my armed forces reservist ID. They told me that I had to report to my army unit within forty-eight hours or serve time in jail for being a military deserter.

The next morning, we were on the train back to Budapest, guarded by armed soldiers at both ends of the coach. Arriving home, we realized that George had a fever from the smallpox vaccination. We called our family doctor, who prescribed some medication, and then I called my father, who was already looking for us. I told him what had happened and that, in spite of everything, we would have to try to escape again. He promised to help us. We went to his brother-in-law Imre's home. Imre had already left the country with his family. We didn't have any money, so I called my next-door neighbour and offered to sell him everything in our apartment for less than 10 per cent of its real value, as we felt we had no other choice.

My father had arranged Imre's escape and now arranged for us to go with the same escort Irme had used. The plan was to travel toward Mosonmagyaróvár with our travel documents, which we still had. One kilometre before the train station, the train would stop, and we were to get off and run to a farm. In the evening, five horse-drawn carriages would take us and other escapees to a point less than one kilometre from the Austrian border. A short walk between watchtowers and we would be free. But it didn't happen that way.

On December 7, 1956, we were on our way. We arrived in the late afternoon at the farm, where George was given warm milk and some food. Darkness fell at 6:00 p.m., and the five carriages arrived. At the same time, a dozen Soviet soldiers showed up and started to round up all those trying to escape. Everybody ran. Vera took our baby and hid, and I ran in the other direction and hid somewhere else. The Soviet soldiers captured many, put them in four of the carriages and took them away. Luckily, the driver of the fifth carriage was able to flee.

When the soldiers left the farm, those who had managed to hide emerged, not knowing who had survived the raid. Vera, holding George, was crying and calling my name. What a happy moment to find each other! The only remaining carriage returned at 8:00 p.m. Six women and some children were put on it. George still had a fever and was crying a lot. We had to give him a small dose of tranquilizer to make him sleepy and quiet. The rest of the group – about a dozen men – marched through the farmer's field in foot-deep mud. Sometimes we had to help the horses pull the carriage.

At midnight, we heard shooting in the village we had just passed, so the owner of the horses didn't want to go any farther. From this point, we all continued on foot. The mud was heavy, and so was George. Vera and I took turns carrying him. At about 4:00 a.m., Vera was carrying George when I fell into a crevice almost two metres deep. I sprained my ankle and didn't think I'd be able to continue, but knowing there was no return, I pushed on, struggling with sharp pain, to reach the border. We passed between watchtowers with bright lights on top. The soldier in the tower had been paid by the escort not to hear or see anything. In this instant, George woke up and said, "Light, light!" It was scary; we had to cover his mouth.

At last, we were in Austria. This part of the border was like a bay, curving deeply into Hungary. Everybody else went to sleep, but the soldiers were too close for comfort, so Vera and I, carrying George, started to walk farther into Austria. We were dead tired, but we wanted to be safe. About thirty minutes into our trek, some people from the Red Cross stopped us and supplied us with some food and dry clothing. We were finally free and ready to face the unknown.

The Red Cross transported us to a refugee camp in Andau, Austria. The floor was covered with straw beds, and the sanitary conditions were poor. The Hungarians we met there openly voiced antisemitic remarks, which brought back awful memories for us. We wanted to get away from there as soon as possible.

Vera knew a couple from Budapest, Elly and Alex Agoston, who had moved to Vienna after the war. We thought they would be able to help us, but unfortunately I didn't have any Austrian money to make a telephone call. My meagre knowledge of German from the Soviet camp helped me ask a well-dressed gentleman for help. His name was Joseph Schwartz, and he was a chemist who owned a pharmaceutical company in Vienna. He called the Agostons at his own expense. Elly was happy to learn that we had left Hungary and told me to come to their house as soon as we could. Mr. Schwartz kindly told us to call him if we needed any help in Vienna.

With the help of the Red Cross, we arrived in Vienna. We called the Agostons, but they were not home, so we went to a Jewish community centre, hoping they could help us. It was Saturday, and the Sabbath service was in progress in the synagogue within the centre. A few Jewish ladies came out of the synagogue and told us they were sorry but, on a Saturday, they could not do much for us. The only food they were able to give us was cold *cholent*, bean stew, but they unfortunately had nothing for George. We had no place to sleep.

Having no other choice, I called Mr. Schwartz and asked for his help in finding a place to stay. He drove us to the outskirts of the city to a refugee camp. He was a big help while we were in Vienna, and we kept in touch with him through cards and letters for the next twenty-five years, informing him of our progress in our new life. He replied every time, delighted that we hadn't forgotten him.

Unfortunately, George was sick. His temperature rose higher every hour, he had diarrhea and he was clearly in pain. He didn't want to eat or drink anything. We had no place to wash him and to make him comfortable. George screamed in pain all night. We called for a doctor. When he saw George, he called an ambulance. George was taken to the St. Anna Children's Hospital, where he was diagnosed with a middle-ear infection.

We had to leave George in the hospital, and we left him there that day with heavy hearts. Vera couldn't stop crying. We were terribly worried about our twenty-month-old son and felt guilty for having left our home and for bringing a small child to the unknown. We had no money and little knowledge of German. It seemed to us then that we had made an irresponsible decision. But we met a young couple in the refugee camp who had left their only child in Hungary in his grandparents' care, and they endured years of heartbreak until they were able to reunite with their child. Leaving our home without George had never even crossed our minds. We wanted to bring up our only child in a better society with more opportunities than he would have had under communist rule.

We had left Budapest with only the clothes on our backs. The Hebrew Immigrant Aid Society (HIAS) gave us some clothes, mostly for George. It was December, and Vienna was decked out with Christmas decorations. The stores were full of merchandise. Vienna, a rich, clean, beautiful city full of well-dressed people, was a stark contrast to Budapest, where there were still clear signs of the impact of World War II and the destruction of the 1956 uprising: buildings full of bullet holes, stores with mostly empty shelves, unaffordable prices on the black market and shortages everywhere. In Budapest we had to buy whatever was available; here there was such abundance and variety, but we had no money. Over time, we realized that we had made the right decision to leave Hungary after all.

The strict rules of the hospital permitted a patient to be visited only once a week. When we went to the hospital sooner than we were allowed to, George was not in his room. In a panic, we ran to the nursing station to find out what had happened to him. A young intern, Dr. Lanik, directed us to another room with twelve beds, where we found George. We hardly recognized him. His head was bandaged, and he looked forlorn among these strangers, who talked to him in German, a language he didn't understand. Crying loudly, he rushed into our arms, and we cried with him.

Dr. Lanik spoke to us about George's condition and informed us that he would have to stay in the hospital for a few weeks. Dr. Lanik saw that not only were we worried, but we were also refugees who needed some help. He told us that his mother had been born in Hungary, and he invited us for supper at his parents' house. Their home was a large apartment with beautiful antique furniture on the outskirts of Vienna. His mother, Susan, greeted us warmly and offered us their bathroom to take a shower. She gave Vera some clothing, promised to wash Vera's clothes and invited us for dinner again the next day. We just couldn't believe our luck, finding such nice people who opened up their home to strangers. We went to the Laniks' house a few more times. We were so grateful for them. We became good friends, and for the next thirty years we exchanged letters, New Year's greetings and family pictures.

Our relatives, mostly Vera's, sent us money to buy food, and we visited a soup kitchen daily. Our friends the Agostons often invited us for lunch or supper. Elly gave some dresses to Vera and insisted on paying for the alterations needed. The HIAS in Vienna did very little to help us. One of the reasons was that we had moved out of the official refugee camp on our own, without their approval. Many people lived in hotel rooms and collected money from the HIAS to purchase food, but we were not smart enough to take advantage of the system. HIAS did give us a little help to get a small room in a hotel. I had to fight for this room, but we felt we really needed our own space in order to care for our son. George was skinny when he was discharged from the hospital, but he was still a beautiful little boy with a lot of curly hair. He had forgotten the few words he knew, but he was happy to be back with us.

In order to obtain refugee visas from the US consulate, we had to provide a sponsorship affidavit from Vera's aunt, Aranka Weltner. We sent a telegram and a letter to her address in New York, which had the house number 9742. In Hungary, the number 7 is written with a short horizontal bar crossing the vertical line. Without that bar, it is read as number 1, so we thought Aranka's house number was 9142. She had never received our letters and therefore hadn't sent any affidavits. On a number of days, I went to shovel the snow at 6:00 a.m. in front of the US consulate so as to be the first in line to enter the registration office. The answer every time: "Sorry! We haven't received anything from your relatives."

In January 1957, the HIAS instructed us to leave the hotel, saying that they were no longer going to pay the bill. We were instructed to move to the city of Korneuburg to an old army camp, where the Swedish Red Cross was taking care of more than one thousand refugees. Our room at the camp housed twenty-four people. As in other army camps, the running water was down the hall. Once a week, we went to the city bathhouse and paid for one hour of bathing facilities. The Agostons came to see us a few times, each time with some food and toys for George.

In the camp, we ate well. So that we could make some extra food for George, we bought a small electric burner. To earn a little money, I went to work in a local shoe factory as a designer. I made several trips to Vienna to the US consulate and the HIAS office, but we didn't seem to be getting any closer to immigrating to the United States. In the meantime, waiting grew increasingly hard. We didn't have any privacy in the camp, and we became depressed.

When my father-in-law learned that we had left Hungary, he too decided to leave his home in Dombóvár with his wife, Elisabeth, and their son, Gabe, who was nine years old at the time. Since the Hungarian border to Austria was already tightly closed, Yugoslavia was the only way to leave Hungary, and they had to cross the frozen Drava River. Their situation was much worse than ours – the Yugoslavian government accepted them as refugees but didn't trust them. We helped them by sending some of the money his sisters had been sending us. From time to time, we sent a food parcel, clothes and some US dollars hidden in cigarette packages.

My mother and sister were glad to hear the news that we were out of Hungary. Naturally, they wanted us to join them in Israel. They resided in the kibbutz of Ein Gev, on the shores of Lake Kinneret. My sister, Barbara, who had divorced her first husband and was now married to a man named Asher, was a member of the kibbutz. Asher was one of the kibbutz truck drivers during weekdays, and on the Sabbath he drove people to the beaches or to other cities. Barbara was working in the garment repair section. My sister's daughters, Hannah and Hava, attended school and day camps. My mother worked half-days in the kitchen.

In my heart, I longed to go to Israel. However, I knew that if we immigrated to Israel, I would be drafted into the army, as well as for follow-up reserve service each year for a month. I didn't want to face the same hardship again in another country, so Israel did not offer an appealing future. We decided that we would wait for the US visas. My mother was unhappy with our plan because she wanted us near her.

Wanting desperately to get out of the camp, Vera went to the Canadian consulate one day to register us to immigrate to Canada. She later explained to me that we had to start our new life and, although family is important, we had to stand on our own feet. I was surprised by her solo decision at the time but, in retrospect, it led to a better life for us.

Although Vera's aunt Aranka lived in New York, she also had relatives in Montreal. One of these relatives, Kate Tarnay, kindly sent us the affidavit taking full financial responsibility for us for one year. A bonus was that the short distance between Montreal and New York would enable us to see Vera's family in New York.

Since both Vera and I had a trade – Vera as a dressmaker and I as a shoemaker – we received our Canadian visas within weeks. We were extremely fortunate that Vera's relatives Aranka, Rose and Katy had bought us airline tickets for a flight that included a stopover in New York. This meant we didn't have to wait for the Canadian government's ship to bring us to Canada. A year later, we repaid these relatives in full.

On June 12, 1957, we flew via Swissair from Austria to Zurich, where we had to wait a few hours while the plane underwent repairs. After a long night, we finally arrived in New York. Every member of Vera's family was waiting outside the gate, waving and crying. Vera had been only eight years old when her aunts Aranka and Rose immigrated to the United States. The Rubins, Vera's cousin Suzy and her husband, obtained special permission for us to delay our connection to Montreal, which enabled us to spend a few hours with them in their home.

The reunion was wonderful. George, of course, was the centre of attention. Before we left for the airport to continue our trip to Montreal, the family generously gave us a wallet containing about two hundred US dollars, which was a sizable amount at that time, to start our new life in Montreal.

Discovering Canada

We arrived at Dorval International Airport in Montreal close to midnight on my lucky day, June 13, 1957. George was asleep, and we were exhausted. In the immigration office, we received our Canadian landing cards and five dollars, our first monthly child allowance. We loved this country right away.

Kate Tarnay, who had sent us the affidavit, welcomed us at the airport. From one of her friends, she rented a room for us – no bigger than a large closet – on Rue de la Peltrie. The next day, we bought a bed and a crib. Our living conditions were pretty meagre. After we registered as newcomers at the federal government office, we were issued food vouchers, each worth $13.50. One voucher was enough for two weeks' worth of food. I used these vouchers on only three occasions. I wanted to work to earn money and not depend on charity. I later paid the government back every penny of the vouchers, even though it wasn't necessary.

A Volkswagen dealer hired me right away. My limited knowledge of German was a plus. I started washing cars for seventy cents per hour and was later promoted to spraying rubber undercoating on new cars. This was a new thing in Canada, but nobody wanted to do it because it was hard, dirty work. It took one hour after work for me to clean up with solvent from the smelly, black material. My pay jumped to ninety cents an hour. I quit the job after six weeks and looked for a job in my trade.

After living for one month on de la Peltrie, we searched for an apartment nearby, but nobody wanted to rent to a couple with a child, unless the apartment was in the basement. The Rubins came up from New York to help us find a suitable apartment, and after a week of looking, we found a one-bedroom on Boulevard Saint-Laurent. The apartment was on the ground floor, and the backyard was dirty. The monthly rent was eighty dollars, and my pay was thirty-five dollars a week. The Rubins brought us a lot of clothing and kitchenware. Vera's aunts, Aranka and Rose, visited us too, and brought linens, blankets and towels. Kate Tarnay gave us a small, second-hand kitchen table and chairs. We were very grateful, and remain so, for all the help we received in starting our new life in Canada.

At first, our furniture was sparse. We used two empty cardboard boxes for night tables until we bought a living-room set on monthly payments. This was the first and last time we bought anything on an instalment plan. Vera's winter coat had been stolen when we arrived at the airport, but since it was summertime and she didn't need a coat, we instead bought a tricycle for George. Every day, Vera took George and his trike to Outremont Park. He usually left his trike in the hallway of our building. One morning, it too was stolen.

We soon took George to a doctor, because he didn't want to eat. He would keep part of the food in his mouth for hours. The pediatrician examined him and found nothing wrong. The huge adjustment to living in a new country and all it entailed caused George not only to lose his appetite, but to delay his first words until he was almost three years old. However, from then on, he spoke in full sentences.

To preserve memories of our new life, I bought a small, used camera for three dollars. We now look back at these black-and-white photos in our family album with joy and pride.

～

In August 1957, I applied for a job at Dependable Slipper and Shoe on Rue St. Paul in Old Montreal. There, I met a Hungarian man, Julius

Horanszky, who had immigrated to Canada with his family when he was eight years old. Since we had been born in the same country, I was his *landsman*. I was hired, and with his support, I learned how to cut leather with a fast-moving machine.

Unfortunately, the other cutters weren't very welcoming. Julius protected me from the antisemitic Ukrainian workers and even some of my fellow Jewish workers. Instead of using my education, previous training and mental faculties, I was doing hard manual labour. With Julius's help, I became a pieceworker like him. We had to punch out on our time cards for the regular working hours, and after that, we were free to work as many hours as we could. This way, the company didn't have to pay overtime. The factory changed its name to Holiday Shoe Corporation five years after I started there and became unionized. This put an end to the old punch-card system, and overtime hours had to be paid.

The factory was cold during the winter and hot in the summer. The building was more than sixty years old, and the heating system was primitive. In the summer, the temperature rose to 35°C. With only a few windows open, there was not much fresh air. When I cut red or black suede, my whole body turned red or black. I smelled like a leather factory, and fellow passengers on the bus ride home kept their distance.

Piecework meant rushing all the time. Going to the bathroom meant lost time and money. Short lunch times, little rest, standing all day and working on the noisy clicker machine were my daily routine. Standing all day long, I developed varicose veins in both legs. I had two painful operations four years apart, easing the pain for a while. However, the varicose veins and the ensuing pain returned. My legs look like a map with many rivers.

The factory produced mostly winter footwear. I earned much less during the off-season in November, December and part of January. To earn extra money, I did delivery for a dry cleaner and drove a taxi, mostly at night. I tried to become my own boss by selling ladies' cardigans and beauty supplies during my free time, but I wasn't a sales-oriented person. I didn't want to lose my steady job for a risky future, so I gave up the idea of becoming my own boss.

On the way to the factory, I learned English from a little pocket dictionary. My goal was to learn one new word a day. Twice a week, I went to evening classes to study English and, later, French. Every other day, Vera took the same classes. Working, having a family life and taking classes was taxing. After supper, when I left for the school, George cried. He wanted me to stay at home and play with him, but learning the language was a compelling reason to leave.

Ten months later, Vera, George and I moved to Barclay Avenue. This was a much better district than Boulevard Saint-Laurent and was closer to an elementary school for George. Meanwhile, we bought a used sewing machine, and Vera started to do clothing alterations. Taking care of George was her priority, but in her free time, Vera earned a few dollars. She worked hard. Her customers were pleased with the quality work and especially her low prices. For a short time, she sewed overcoat linings for a coat factory. The pay was only nine cents per piece. That amounted to three dollars for a day's work, but we never complained; we were just happy to make ends meet.

In 1958, after more than a year in Yugoslavia, Vera's father, Jozsef, and his family were able to immigrate to the United States. His two sisters took good care of them. They helped him, Elisabeth and Gabe find an apartment in New York City, in the Bronx, and furnished it completely. As Gabe grew up, he always helped the whole family. He was a caring, wonderful son to his parents and is a loving brother to Vera. After graduating from Pratt Institute, Gabe became a talented industrial designer and started his own company. As an adult, besides his work and taking care of his three children, he spent a lot of time looking after his elderly aunt, Aranka. Elisabeth went to work in the same factory as her relatives. Jozsef took a job at the Otis Elevator Company and loved his new country and the improved living conditions. He and his family often drove to Canada to visit us, and we spent countless summer holidays together. Jozsef was an intelligent man who loved music and played the violin. I respected him for his devotion to his family and his good advice.

Montreal had a large Hungarian population, and we eventually discovered some other people we knew from the camp in Korneuburg, including Ervin Reiner and his mother, Margit. It was also a surprise to find my buddy Jozsi Kohn from the Soviet camp, who had changed his name to Komlos after he came back to Budapest, which was why I hadn't been able to find him. Vera reunited with her childhood friend Eva Kertesz and her husband, George, and their lovely daughter, Georgina. We went to the beaches or riverside in the summer with our friends. They all had small children, so George had lots of playmates.

In 1959, I bought a blue Chevrolet for $350. We occasionally drove to Missisquoi Bay, on the Canadian side of Lake Champlain, close to the US border. Our new car played an important role in keeping us in touch with our relatives in New York. Since there was no superhighway then, the trip took twelve long hours, but we had so much fun together. We once met Gabe, Aranka and Elisabeth in Saratoga Springs, New York, and drove them to Montreal for a vacation. When we could afford to, we took a few short, simple vacations, sometimes with our family from New York, to a small village called Saint-Gabriel-de-Brandon, or to the Laurentians or the Catskills. Apart from enjoying our car on the trips we took, I saved travelling time to my workplace and to the stores.

In 1958, we invited my mother to visit us in Montreal. My sister, Barbara, had stopped communicating with us for a while because she was disappointed that we hadn't come to Israel. Only my mother answered our letters. I took care of obtaining a Canadian visa for her while she applied for a passport. My mother was an honest person. She told the Israeli officials in the passport office, when they asked, that my father had divorced her. Since the divorce had been obtained in Hungary, it was not considered legal under Israeli law. According to the law at the time, a husband had to apply for a passport, or a loan, for his wife. My father was furious when my mother asked him to obtain an official divorce, which required him to declare his intention in front of a rabbinical court. This kind of religious ritual could create a problem for him in communist Hungary. Although he agreed, it took a long time and delayed my mother's departure from Israel to Canada. In early June of 1959, she received a Canadian visa for one year.

Waiting for my mother at the airport gave me the feeling that I was turning another page in my history book. A tired, nervous little lady walked out with a small suitcase. The crying, hugging and kissing lasted a long time. Seeing me for the first time in almost fifteen years and Vera and little George for the first time ever was very emotional for her. On the way home, George asked, "Dad, is she really your mother? You don't look like her!" My mother looked years older than her chronological age – nineteen difficult years of marriage to my father, hiding with my sister on a farm during the war and three years in Europe as a refugee had all taken a heavy toll on her health.

That August, my mother's brother Alex, his wife, Sara, and their daughter, Joan, came to Montreal from Brooklyn to visit my mother. That was some reunion! Alex and my mother had last seen each other in 1937, before he immigrated to the United States. Before my mother returned to Israel, she visited their family in Brooklyn.

My mother seemed comfortable with us, but she had a heart condition and sometimes felt sick. I was unhappy that my mother smoked heavily – her heart condition meant she should not have smoked at all. And after the mild climate in Israel, the Canadian winter was difficult for her. She never stopped talking about my sister, Barbara, and her four children: two daughters, Hannah and Hava, from her first marriage, and two sons, Rony and Ejal, from her marriage to Asher. On the kibbutz, my mother often took care of Barbara and Asher's children while they worked. She was very close to her grandchildren, and she felt that without her care, the children couldn't live a normal life. Even when they were grown up, my mother had a major influence on them, which created friction between my sister and my mother.

My mother was a great help to us, cooking and baking, and she taught George Hungarian. Vera loved her, made her dresses and bought her all kinds of clothes. But after nine months away from the other side of her family, my mother was restless. In March of 1960, with tears in her eyes, she returned to Israel. We were sorry to see her leave.

When my mother arrived at the kibbutz, Barbara surprised her with the news that they were going to leave because they didn't like living in the kibbutz anymore. It was not a simple move to make. As long as they were members of the kibbutz, they had everything they needed, owning only their personal belongings. My mother wanted to stay, but since she wasn't a member, she had to leave, too. They rented a small apartment in Petah Tikva. Asher took a job as a truck driver for an oil company in Haifa. Barbara worked at home as a dressmaker for well-to-do people who paid cash for her work. When she retired, she didn't have a pension. As we sent Barbara's family parcels and helped them out financially, my relationship with my sister improved.

⌒

George attended kindergarten and four elementary grades at École Bedford. By Grade 2, already an independent boy, George walked to school and back without his mother. He was also very honest. One day, he went alone to the barbershop near our apartment. Haircuts at that time cost ninety cents, so I gave him one dollar. When he came back, he said, "You know, Dad, I had so much hair that I was afraid the barber would ask for more than ninety cents. He didn't. I was so happy that I gave him a ten-cent tip."

On September 14, 1962, Vera, George and I all became Canadian citizens. We appreciated that Canada had welcomed us with open arms. In 1965, we moved to a fourth-floor apartment on Avenue Bourret that had a large living room, a kitchen with a window, and two bedrooms, so that George could have his own room. Vera continued to work for a high-class women's clothing store doing alterations. She spent three days a week in the store doing fittings and brought home the dresses, coats and suits to work on for the other days. It was not easy taking care of George, the household and doing her work. She often went to sleep after midnight because she had to finish the alterations. Vera was, and is, a perfectionist, and more and more customers wanted her work.

After working in the clothing store for six years, Vera fell ill with hepatitis, and had to stop working in the store. When she had fully recovered, the Magnasonic Company, which later became Sanyo Canada, hired her. She had less income than she had working for the clothing store, but also less stress. Vera worked in the accounting/ credit departments for the next nineteen years, until the company moved to Toronto.

On May 4, 1968, an important event took place: George's bar mitzvah. The Young Israel of Montreal synagogue opened the door for our more than one hundred guests – our Montreal friends and our relatives from the United States. George said his part of the Haftorah and gave a short speech. A lunch followed the service, and then we invited the out-of-town guests for dinner at an elegant restaurant.

My mother could not come for George's bar mitzvah, so I instead arranged to see her during my summer vacation. My flight was delayed for nine hours in Montreal because of engine failure, and I didn't arrived at Tel Aviv Airport until after midnight. I was surprised to see my sister, her husband and her four children waiting for me. The last time I had seen my sister was in 1944, when she was a young girl. Now, in 1968, she was a woman with four children. Although there had been lots of family reunions at the airport, this was probably one of the loudest and longest.

When we arrived at their house, my mother was waiting for me with tears and open arms. She had aged a lot, become more nervous and smoked even more than before. Over the following two weeks, we talked and ate a great deal. I wanted to get acquainted with Barbara and her children, and they wanted to know all about Vera and George. Sometimes everybody talked at the same time, but we understood one another well. They took me to the beaches and famous sites, and we visited friends or relatives in the evenings. I don't have the words to express the feelings I had when I had to say goodbye, especially to my mother. I wondered if I would ever see her or my sister again.

~

Like Vera and me, George was ambitious and hard-working. He found work every summer, whether at a Laurentian summer camp, the Jasper Park Lodge in the Rockies in Alberta, or at Homowack Lodge in the Catskill Mountains.

In 1972, when Vera received some restitution money from the German government, we decided to spend this money on a trip to Israel as a university graduation present for George. I was thrilled that I would be able to see my family again, and that Barbara and her family would finally meet Vera and George. In the summer of 1972, we spent an unforgettable three weeks in Israel. I had to return to Montreal for work, but Vera and George took a detour to Budapest for a week. After sixteen years, my father and his wife, Margit, were delighted to see George.

In 1975, to our great pleasure, George was accepted into McGill University's Faculty of Medicine. Vera and I did our utmost to ensure George could study in a quiet atmosphere. He kept us abreast of his studies and friends, and we remained a close-knit family. George met a lovely Jewish girl, Joanie Birnbaum, who was studying occupational therapy, also at McGill. They became engaged in September of 1978.

My father-in-law, who had had a heart attack and bypass surgery, came to Montreal for George's engagement party, even in his weakened condition. This was his last visit to our home. Joe passed away in February 1979, at seventy-five years of age. I think of him often and sometimes read the beautiful poems he wrote about his family and nature while at his favourite beach, Jones Beach in Long Island, New York. Vera's stepmother, Elisabeth, had been sick often since being liberated from the concentration camp. She had cancer, developed osteoporosis and had emphysema. She suffered for several years before she passed away, also at the age of seventy-five.

George and Joanie got married in May of 1979. Three days after the wedding, another big event took place: George's convocation ceremony. He became Dr. Vertes! Vera and I, Holocaust survivors and hard-working immigrants, were such proud parents; our son had fulfilled our wildest dream.

Joanie and George moved to Toronto, where George did his specialty training in cardiology. Without George, our home was too quiet. We missed all the discussions and activities with our son. To our great delight, George and Joanie's son, Gregory, was born on May 29, 1986. When they brought him home from the hospital, we were there to greet our new grandson. Their beautiful little girl, Jaclyn, was born on August 3, 1989. While Vera and I were in Florida in the harsh winter of 1995, Joanie gave birth to Alex on February 15. We flew to Toronto immediately upon hearing the great news.

Now, it is our great pride and pleasure to see our grandchildren growing up and working hard in university. We are so happy that, being born in Canada, they have their parents and grandparents in their lives, and we hope they will have peaceful, successful lives.

~

On July 13, 1980, my mother died at the age of seventy-five. I rushed to make travel plans so I could attend the funeral in Petah Tikva. I sat shiva with my sister and spoke with the many family members and friends of my mother's. I already missed her, and knew I would miss reading her warm letters.

After my mother's funeral, I took a detour to Budapest because Vera insisted that I visit my father. Vera had developed a good relationship with him after George was born, and we had kept in regular contact with him from Montreal. I sent him razor blades, antihistamine and other items he needed. We exchanged postage stamps for each other's collection. Although twenty-four years had passed since I had last seen him, my father had not changed much. I hugged him and kissed Margit. They invited me to dinner. My father started the meal with brandy and continued with wine and beer. We took a taxi to downtown Budapest to visit the newly opened Vigadó Concert Hall.

I visited my father and Margit the following Thursday. However, for the past two years my father had had a standing appointment with a dermatologist on Thursdays, and he didn't think my visit was a sufficient reason to miss it. Margit begged him to skip this unimportant visit and spend a few more hours with me. He did not say anything, just shook my hand and left. I was speechless. Margit apologized for his rudeness. I watched my father turn the corner and not look back. I was obviously not important to him; I was only his son. Our visit reminded me of the time I had visited him in the hospital after his gallbladder surgery; again he treated me like a stranger, not like his son. I hope that I have been a more caring father to my son.

Margit died that same year from complications following hip surgery. My father retired a few years later. My sister, Barbara, came from Israel to help my father adjust and to organize his household. They had a lot of arguments, so a month later, she returned home.

I continued to correspond with my father, sending him whatever he asked for. My father died of liver disease on January 16, 1990. His friend Stephan told me that my father had arranged his own funeral in advance and that he had been buried the day following his death. He had lived without his children and he died without them.

~

In 1995, we went to Israel to visit my sister and her growing family. Placing flowers on my mother's grave was very emotional for me. We enjoyed travelling to the Dead Sea and Eilat and to visit my sister's son Ron and his family on a moshav. Since my last visit in 1980, Israel had grown into a beautiful, modern country.

From Israel, we proceeded to Hungary. My uncle Erno had passed away there four years earlier. When we visited Vera's mother's grave in Dombóvár, we were sorry to see the neglected condition of the cemetery. Like most of the small cities in Hungary, Dombóvár presently has no Jewish inhabitants, and nobody takes care of the Jewish cemetery there. In Budapest, we visited my father's well-kept grave. Facing his tombstone, I felt that a chapter of my life had come to an end.

Epilogue

I worked at the shoe factory for twenty-eight years, thirteen of those as a cutter, and then as foreman. My job included supervising the production, teaching new cutters and looking after the stockroom. I had to calculate both material and labour costs. I devised a new system of calculating productivity by applying the knowledge from my Hungarian work experience and presented it to management and to the labour union. My new system was a success.

The International Footwear Association sent two industrial engineers from its head office to study my system, which subsequently became the basis for every footwear manufacturer. I received a special bonus for my work. When the computer revolution began, the company was the first to computerize its whole factory, from sales to shipping. The programmers didn't know anything about footwear, so I provided the technical details. Simultaneously, I started to learn computer basics, which was enjoyable. The owner of the company later offered me a position in the office, doing cost calculations and teaching other employees how to use the computer. For the next five years, I kept busy in the main office.

Unfortunately, the sales department wanted to sell the footwear at the lowest possible price. For the previous thirty years, the company's operation had been profitable, putting it in a position to buy new machinery and install assembly lines. New management, however, made risky decisions and lost money on expenditures. It did not come as a surprise to me when the bank audited the company's books and called in their loan immediately. The company was unable to pay back the outstanding loan and had no choice but to declare bankruptcy. The trustee who took over the property of this fine company had to sell off all the footwear, materials and equipment to recover some money.

After giving my all to this company for twenty-eight years, I received only one week's salary and not a penny of severance pay. I was sixty years old, without a job. I mailed my resumé to close to fifty different companies, without any success. While I had been working, I had had tons of job offers, but now no one wanted to give me a chance. My hope, my bank account and my spirit were all at a low point, and I became a bit depressed. We had just bought a condominium, and I had planned to work until the age of sixty-five to save enough money to complete the furnishing of our home and have enough for retirement. Gabe, my brother-in-law, restored my confidence. He told me not to lose hope and that should I ever need help, he would have my back. I am, indeed, lucky to have him in my life. He is the most wonderful brother-in-law anybody could have.

Kate's Sport Company eventually hired me to sell their overproduction and returns. Although I knew little about textiles or women's styles, I became an expert in a short period of time. The store was successful, although when the lease expired at the end of one year, it closed. I next organized after-season sales in the company's factory, with even greater success. Sometimes I hired more than a dozen salespeople. I enjoyed the job. My knowledge of French and computers helped me get a job for a sewing machine importer for the next few years.

When I turned sixty-five, Vera and I analyzed our financial situation, and we decided that the time had come for me to retire. I kept busy fixing up our home. Although it was new, there were always things to repair or improve. Vera was sixty-two years old when she happily retired and became an early pensioner. Over the years, we were lucky to have been able to travel to many different countries. We had celebrated our twenty-fifth anniversary in Hawaii, our fiftieth in western Canada, and had been to Spain, London, Paris, Switzerland and Italy. During our retirement years, we spent the winters in Florida to escape the harsh weather, until our health worsened and we needed frequent medical attention. Now, we "enjoy" the difficult winters in Montreal.

~

The positive side to my life story was crossing the ocean to Canada, where I made a new home with my wife, Vera, and son, George. Vera and I worked hard to provide our son with a good life and the opportunity to pursue an education and various interests. If I had the chance to go back in time and pick any place to live, I would choose Canada all over again.

If I had a chance to start my life all over again, there are some things I would do differently. However, there are certain things I would never change: I would marry my Vera. Nobody else could be a better wife and friend to me. I would have a son exactly like George. No other child could have given me as much pleasure from the time he was born to seeing his progress day by day. I am blessed with three wonderful grandchildren. My son, George, and my daughter-in-law, Joanie, share my gratitude for our enlarged family tree. Our family circle is very small, as it is for many Holocaust survivors. The Holocaust took away so many members of our family; so many of us were alone in the storm. We treasure the precious few who are left.

During my lifetime, countless people helped me. During my retirement, it was my turn to help others. I volunteered for various organizations, helping out with the Israel Day celebration in Montreal, Combined Jewish Appeal fundraising, March to Jerusalem celebrations and the Montreal Holocaust Memorial Centre's many activities. Later, I became one of the centre's regular speakers, sharing my experiences as a Holocaust survivor with students. So far, I have made eighty-four presentations, reaching close to six thousand mostly non-Jewish students.

After my tenth visit to share my experiences with students at Champlain College in Saint-Lambert, I received an honorary World Studies Certificate. Because I was unable to finish the fourth year of high school in Hungary due to the Jewish quota, the certificate meant a lot to me.

For five years, I was elected to the Montreal Holocaust Memorial Centre's Board of Directors. In 2000, I took on extra volunteer work at the Cummings Jewish Centre for Seniors, helping survivors to obtain compensation from different countries. I also participated in committees in our condominium building. In 2001, I was the first person to receive the Merit Award from Le Vicomte Condominium Association. In 2013, I received the Holocaust Memorial Centre Award. In 2015, I was honoured with two awards – Quebec's YMCA Peace Medal and the Governor General's Caring Canadian Award from His Excellency the Right Honourable David Johnston, in recognition of my volunteerism and contributions to the community.

Poem

MEMORIAL CANDLE

Watching the memorial candle's flickering light,
You try to remember many events, the dark and the bright.
There is only one candle burning on your table
And you want to start a prayer, but you are not able.

Yisgadal
There should be a dozen candles, thousands or millions more
To put on every table, in every home, even to cover the entire floor.
But you light up one candle and look into its flame,
Being a survivor, you know very well whom to blame.

Yisgadal v'yiskadash
The memories will be here forever to stay,
Our pain and emptiness will never go away.
Still the Earth is moving, still the clock is ticking,
Still we keep crying, but we must go on living!

Today followed yesterday, tomorrow will be the day after.
Give yourself peace of mind, a hopeful time. Now, not later!
Today your tears are flowing when you pray.
Tomorrow you will have a better day.

Yisgadal v'yiskadash sh'mei
Life can't be controlled only by your past,
Think about your future, that is a must!
We have to take care of our friends and family;
Think about it. We have to fulfill our destiny.

Look again into the cool, blue candlelight,
And look ahead for a brand new fight.
So, my friend, say one more time:
Yisgadal v'yiskadash sh'mei raba.

    Leslie Vertes

Glossary

antisemitism Prejudice, discrimination, persecution and/or hatred against Jewish people, institutions, culture and symbols.

Arrow Cross Party (in Hungarian, Nyilaskeresztes Párt – Hungarista Mozgalom; abbreviation: Nyilas) A Hungarian nationalistic and antisemitic party founded by Ferenc Szálasi in 1935 under the name the Party of National Will. With the full support of Nazi Germany, the newly renamed Arrow Cross Party ran in Hungary's 1939 election and won 25 per cent of the vote. The party was banned shortly after the elections, but was legalized again in March 1944 when Germany occupied Hungary. Under Nazi approval, the party assumed control of Hungary from October 15, 1944, to March 1945, led by Szálasi under the name the Government of National Unity. The Arrow Cross regime was particularly brutal – during their short period of rule, they instigated the murder of tens of thousands of Hungarian Jews. Between December 1944 and January 1945, the Arrow Cross murdered approximately 20,000 Jews, many of whom had been forced into a closed ghetto at the end of November 1944. *See also* Budapest ghetto.

ÁVO (Hungarian; acronym for Magyar Államrendőrség Államvédelmi Osztály, the Hungarian State Security Department) A branch of the Soviet secret police that operated in Hungary from 1946 to 1956, the ÁVO was brutally violent and much feared. During the Hungarian Revolution in 1956, rebels sought revenge, killing many of the officers of ÁVO and informants who worked for them.

Budapest ghetto The area established by the government of Hungary on November 29, 1944. By December 10, the ghetto and its 33,000 Jewish inhabitants were sealed off from the rest of the city. At the end of December, Jews who had previously held "protected" status (many by the Swedish government) were moved into the ghetto and the number of residents increased to 55,000; by January 1945, the number had reached 70,000. The ghetto was overcrowded and lacked sufficient food, water and sanitation. Supplies dwindled and conditions worsened during the Soviet siege of Budapest and thousands died of starvation and disease. Soviet forces liberated the ghetto on January 18, 1945.

Communist Party of Hungary First founded in 1918 and resurrected in 1945 following the liberation and occupation of Hungary by the Soviet Union. The Party was assisted both openly and clandestinely by the USSR and initially had the support of many Hungarians who had opposed the wartime pro-Nazi government in Hungary. The Communist Party merged with the Social Democratic Party in 1948 and was renamed the Hungarian Working People's Party and then, in 1956, the Hungarian Socialist Workers' Party; it consolidated total power in Hungary by 1949, which it held until 1989. *See also* Hungarian Uprising.

DP camps Facilities set up by the Allied authorities and the United Nations Relief and Rehabilitation Administration (UNRRA) in October 1945 to resolve the refugee crisis that arose at the end of World War II. The camps provided temporary shelter and assistance to the millions of people – not only Jews – who had been displaced from their home countries as a result of the war and helped them prepare for resettlement.

Endre, László (1895–1946) The antisemitic deputy prefect of Pest County who became the secretary of state in 1944, heading the administrative section of the Hungarian Ministry of the Interior.

Endre collaborated with the Nazis by drafting a decree that outlined the procedures to be followed and implemented in rounding up the Jewish population into ghettos and deporting Jews to
concentration and death camps. After the war, Endre was tried
and executed in Budapest.

fifth column A term first used by the Nationalists in the Spanish
Civil War of 1936–1939 to refer to their supporters within the ter-
ritories controlled by the Republican side. Because these people
were helping the four columns of the Nationalists' army, they were
deemed to be their "fifth column." Since that time, the expression
has been used to designate a group of people who are clandestinely collaborating with an invading enemy.

gimnázium (Hungarian; in German, *Gymnasium*) A word used
throughout central and eastern Europe to denote high school or
secondary school.

Haftorah The portion read from the Book of Prophets after the Torah
reading at Sabbath services and major festivals; it is traditionally
sung by the youth who is celebrating his or her bar/bat mitzvah.

Hebrew Immigrant Aid Society (HIAS) An organization founded in New York in 1881 that continues to provide aid, counsel,
support and general assistance to Jewish immigrants all over the
world. Since the early 1970s, HIAS has been especially active in
providing assistance to Jews emigrating from the USSR.

Horthy, Miklós (1868–1957) The regent of Hungary during the interwar period and for much of World War II. Horthy presided over
a government that was aligned with the Axis powers and supported Nazi ideology. After the German army occupied Hungary in
March 1944, Horthy served primarily as a figurehead to the pro-
Nazi government; nevertheless, he was able to order the suspen-
sion of the deportation of Hungarian Jews to death camps in the
beginning of July 1944. Horthy planned to withdraw his country
from the war on October 15, 1944, but the Nazis supported an Arrow Cross coup that same day and forced Horthy to abdicate.

Hungarian Revolution (1956) A spontaneous uprising against the Soviet-backed communist government of Hungary in October 1956, the Hungarian Revolution led to the brief establishment of a reformist government under Prime Minister Imre Nagy. The revolution was swiftly crushed by the Soviet invasion of November 1956, during which thousands of civilians were killed. *See also* Nagy, Imre.

Klar, Dr. Zoltan (1894–1966) A physician, journalist and editor of the Hungarian newspaper *Társadalmunk* (Our Society). During World War II, Klar was imprisoned at Mauthausen and was appointed head of medical staff by the Nazis, who wanted to deceive a visiting Red Cross delegation into thinking adequate medical care was available to prisoners. After the war, Klar founded a Budapest agency to assist Jewish concentration camp survivors and later was editor of a Hungarian-language weekly newspaper in New York.

landsman A Yiddish term referring to a Jew who comes from the same town or area as another Jew.

Levente (abbreviation of Levente Egyesületek; Hungarian; literally, knight) A paramilitary youth corps established in Hungary in 1921. Youth between the ages of twelve and twenty-one were obliged to join the organization during World War II and underwent military training and service.

machorka (Russian) Homegrown tobacco.

March to Jerusalem An annual community walk organized to show support for Israel and raise funds for Jewish and Israeli community services.

moshav (Hebrew; literally, settlement or village) An agricultural cooperative comprised of individually-owned farms that was founded by the Labour Zionist movement in the early twentieth century.

Munkaszolgálat (Hungarian; Labour Service) Hungary's military-related labour service system, which was first established in 1919 for those considered too "politically unreliable" for regular military service. After the labour service was made compulsory in 1939, Jewish men of military age were recruited to serve; however, having been deemed "unfit" to bear arms, they were equipped with tools and employed in mining, road and rail construction and maintenance work. Though the men were treated relatively well at first, the system became increasingly punitive in nature. By 1941, Jews in forced labour battalions were required to wear a yellow armband and civilian clothes; they had no formal rank and were unarmed; they were often mistreated by extremely antisemitic supervisors; and their work included clearing minefields, causing their death. Between 20,000 and 40,000 Jewish men died during their forced labour service.

Nagy, Imre (1896–1958) Prime minister of Hungary from July 1953 to April 1955 and from October 24 to November 4, 1956. During his first tenure as prime minister, Nagy went against communist policy by attempting to release political prisoners and bring in economic reforms. Expelled from his position by the Communist Party, he was reinstated in 1956, following popular support during the Hungarian Uprising. Nagy withdrew Hungary from the Warsaw Pact and was subsequently arrested by the Soviets, who executed him after a secret trial in 1958. In 1989, Imre Nagy was given a formal, public funeral, and was recognized as a hero of the Hungarian Uprising.

NKVD (Russian) The acronym of the Narodnyi Komissariat Vnutrennikh Del, meaning People's Commissariat for Internal Affairs. The NKVD functioned as the Soviet Union's security agency, secret police and intelligence agency from 1934 to 1954. The NKVD's Main Directorate for State Security (GUGB) was the forerunner of the Committee for State Security, better known as the KGB (acronym for Komitet Gosudarstvennoy Bezopasnosti) established in 1954. The organization's stated dual purpose was to defend the USSR from external dangers from foreign powers and to protect the Communist Party from perceived dangers within. Under Soviet leader Joseph Stalin, the pursuit of imagined conspiracies

against the state became a central focus and the NKVD played a
critical role in suppressing political dissent.

Oberscharführer (German; senior squad leader) A Nazi SS party
rank between 1932 and 1945. *See also* SS.

partisans Members of irregular military forces or resistance move-
ments formed to oppose armies of occupation. During World
War II there were a number of different partisan groups that opposed both the Nazis and their collaborators in several countries.
The term "partisan" could include highly organized, almost paramilitary groups such as the Red Army partisans; ad hoc groups
bent more on survival than resistance; and roving groups of ban-
dits who plundered what they could from all sides during the war.

POW camp A site where enemy fighters are kept during times of war.
POW camps are supposed to be governed by the Third Geneva
Convention, which requires that the camps be open to inspec-
tion by neutral third parties and outlines the protections offered
to prisoners of war.

Raynaud's disease A rare disorder affecting the circulation of blood
when an individual is exposed to cold or is stressed. The affected
areas, often the fingers and toes, turn white and blue and may
become numb. When the blood flow returns, the skin turns red
and throbs or tingles.

Schutzpass (German; pl. *Schutzpässe*; protective pass) A visa that
identified the holder as a Swedish subject. Swedish diplomat Raoul
Wallenberg issued these passes to at least 15,000 Hungarian Jews,
thereby saving them from deportation. *See also* Wallenberg, Raoul.

shiva (Hebrew; literally, seven) In Judaism, the seven-day mourning
period that is observed after the funeral of a close relative.

SS (abbreviation of Schutzstaffel; Defence Corps). The SS was established in 1925 as Adolf Hitler's elite corps of personal bodyguards.
Under the direction of Heinrich Himmler, its membership grew
from 280 in 1929 to 50,000 when the Nazis came to power in 1933,
and to nearly a quarter of a million on the eve of World War II.

The SS was comprised of the Allgemeine-SS (General SS) and the Waffen-SS (Armed, or Combat SS). The General SS dealt with policing and the enforcement of Nazi racial policies in Germany and the Nazi-occupied countries. The SS ran the concentration and death camps, with all their associated economic enterprises, and also fielded its own Waffen-SS military divisions, including some recruited from the occupied countries.

Tito, Josip Broz (1892–1980) The commander of the Yugoslav Partisans between 1941 and 1945, and president of Yugoslavia between 1953 and 1980. During World War II, Tito sided with the Allies and led an anti-fascist resistance movement that comprised various ethnicities, including Jews.

Treaty of Trianon One of the five treaties produced at the 1919 Paris Peace Conference organized by the victors of World War I. The Treaty of Trianon imposed a harsh peace on Hungary, exacting reparations and redrawing its borders so that Hungary lost over two-thirds of its territory and about two-thirds of its inhabitants.

Wallenberg, Raoul (1912–1947?) The Swedish diplomat who was sent to Hungary in June 1944 by the US Refugee Board and succeeded in saving tens of thousands of Budapest Jews by issuing them Swedish certificates of protection. Of the slightly more than 100,000 Jews who remained alive in Budapest at the end of the war (out of a pre-war population of 247,000), the majority were saved through his efforts. Wallenberg was awarded the title of Righteous Among the Nations by Yad Vashem in 1986 and has been honoured by memorials or monuments in ten other countries. *See also* Schutzpass.

Wehrmacht (German) The German army during the Third Reich.

yisgadal v'yiskadash sh'mei raba (Aramaic; literally, magnified and sanctified be His great name) The opening words of the Mourner's Prayer, also known as Kaddish, said in praise of God as part of mourning rituals in Jewish prayer services, as well as at funerals and memorials.

Photographs

1 Leslie Vertes, age 4 (right), with a friend. Kisvárda, 1928.
2 Leslie (far left), on a hike with friends. Budapest, 1939.

1

2

1 The Winkler family before the war. From left to right: Leslie's mother, Ilona; his sister, Borka; Leslie; and Leslie's father, Sándor. Budapest, 1940.

2 Leslie with his mother (right), and sister (left). Budapest, 1942.

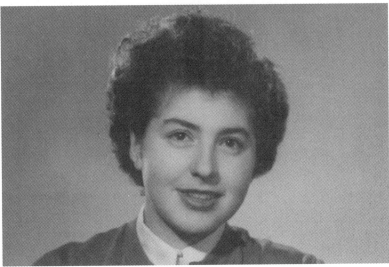

1 Leslie in Budapest after his liberation.
2 Leslie's fiancée, Vera Neiser. Budapest, 1951.

1   Vera's mother, Elisabeth, 1926.
2   Vera's father, Jozsef. Dombóvár, 1942.
3   The only photo of Vera (left) with her sisters before the war. Circa 1940.

1

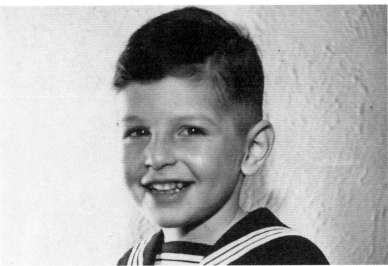

2

1 Leslie and Vera. Budapest, 1954.
2 Leslie and Vera's son, George. 1959.

1 Reunion of Leslie and his mother, Ilona, fifteen years after the war. Montreal, 1959.

2 Vera, Ilona, Leslie and George. Montreal, 1959.

3 Ilona and her brother Alex, who hadn't seen one another for twenty-two years. Montreal, 1959.

4 Leslie's father, Sándor, with his wife, Margit. Budapest, 1960.

1 Leslie with his sister, Borka (Barbara), twenty-four years after they said goodbye to one another in Budapest. Israel, 1968.

2 Leslie's mother, Ilona. Israel, 1977.

3 Leslie (right) with his uncle Erno and aunt Anna. Budapest, 1972.

1 Vera's father, Jozsef, and his second wife, Elisabeth. New York, 1975.

2 Vera with her brother, Gabe. 1998.

3 Leslie's sister, Barbara (front, centre) with her husband and her children in Israel, 1998. Back row, left to right: Ron; his wife, Ofra; Asher; Ejal; and Ejal's wife, Nurit. In front, left to right: David; Hannah; Barbara; Hava; and Haim.

1 Leslie and Vera with their grandchildren, Gregory, Jaclyn and Alex. Toronto, 1990s.
2 Gregory, Alex and Jaclyn. Toronto, 1999.
3 Gregory and Alex, 2011.
4 Jaclyn, 2011.

1 The Vertes' generations: Leslie (third from left) with his son, George, and his grandsons, Gregory and Alex. Toronto, 2002.

2 Leslie and his son, George, at a friend's wedding, 2005.

3 Leslie's son, George, and his family on their way to a wedding. From left to right: George, Alex, Joanie, Gregory and Jaclyn. Toronto, 2009.

Leslie speaking to a group of students at Champlain College (CEGEP). Saint-Lambert, Quebec, 2011.

Leslie and Vera in Toronto, 2002.

Leslie Vertes, 2012.

Index

The Azrieli Foundation was established in 1989 to realize and extend the philanthropic vision of David J. Azrieli, C.M., C.Q., M.Arch. The Foundation's mission is to support a wide spectrum of initiatives in education and research. The Azrieli Foundation is an active supporter of programs in the fields of Education, the education of architects, scientific and medical research, and the arts. The Azrieli Foundation's many initiatives include: the Holocaust Survivor Memoirs Program, which collects, preserves, publishes and distributes the written memoirs of survivors in Canada; the Azrieli Institute for Educational Empowerment, an innovative program successfully working to keep at-risk youth in school; the Azrieli Fellows Program, which promotes academic excellence and leadership on the graduate level at Israeli universities; the Azrieli Music Project, which celebrates and fosters the creation of high-quality new Jewish orchestral music; and the Azrieli Neurodevelopmental Research Program, which supports advanced research on neurodevelopmental disorders, particularly Fragile X and Autism Spectrum Disorders.